Protecting Human Rights in Infoage

Protecting Human Rights in Infoage

Alok Chakravarti

Reference Press

4831/24, Ansari Road
Darya Ganj
New Delhi-110 002
Phone: 3260807
Fax: 3274173
E-mail: essess@del3.vsnl.net.in

First Published 2003

ISBN: 81-88583-02-2

Price: Rs.600/-

Published by:
Reference Press
4831/24, Ansari Road,
Darya Ganj,
New Delhi-110 002.
Phone: 3260807
Fax: 3274173
E-mail: essess@del3.vsnl.net.in

Printed in India by:
Mehra Offset Press

CONTENTS

Preface

The Universal Declaration of Human Rights set out two principles that bear directly on the protection of rights in the digital age. Article 12 of the UDHR states that "No one shall be subjected to arbitrary interference with his privacy, family, home or correspondence, nor to attacks upon his honour and reputation. Everyone has the right to the protection of the law against such interference or attacks." Article 19 further says "Everyone has the right to freedom of opinion and expression; this right includes freedom to hold opinions without interference and to seek, receive and impart information and ideas through any media and regardless of frontiers.

New technology offers opportunities both to expand and to limit the freedom to communicate and the opportunity to protect private life. They enables anonymous transactions over the internet so that individuals can obtain access to information and purchase products without disclosing actual identity. They have significantly influence the future of human rights on the digital age, technical organizations are playing an increasingly significant role in the policy world. They have always presented opportunities and risks. Industrialization promoted productivity and increased the standard of living in many parts of the world. Industrialization also caused enormous damage to the physical environment. Information technology also presents opportunity and risk. But the main challenges to human rights in the digital age is not in the nature of the technology itself but in the capacity of individuals acting through democratic institutions to respond effectively to these new challenges. These new challenges include the commercialization of the Internet, the growth of law enforcement authority, and the globalization of decision-making authority. There is also a critical need to understand the appropriate relationship between the two central interests of privacy and free expression.

To safeguard the rights of privacy and freedom of expression in the digital age, it is necessary to reaffirm support for the Universal Declaration of Human Rights, particularly Article 12 and Article 19; promote the implementation of "Fair Information Practices" and the development of genuine Privacy Enhancing Technologies; remove barriers to the free flow of information; and encourage the participation of "Public Voice" NGOs in decisions concerning the future of the Internet society.

This book attempts to describe the state of human rights in the digitised world. It will serve as a beneficial reference tool for administrators, policy planners, students, teachers, human rights activists and the concrened.

1

Introduction

The Universal Declaration of Human Rights makes clear the need to safeguard the rights of privacy and freedom of expression in the digital age. But new technologies pose new challenges to these essential rights.

Interactive technology makes possible widespread surveillance of private activity. Software filters can also restrict access to information that might otherwise be freely available in the environment of broadcast media and print publication.

Globalization has also resulted in a transfer of decision-making authority from national governments to international organizations.

These recent developments pose additional challenges to democratic institutions and the rule of law. To preserve human dignity it is necessary to reaffirm support for the UDHR, promote the implementation of "Fair Information Practices" and the development of genuine Privacy Enhancing Technologies, remove barriers to the free flow of information, and strengthen "Public Voice" NGOs to ensure the participation of civil society in decisions concerning the digital age.

Present Situation

The Universal Declaration of Human Rights (1948) set out two principles that bear directly on the protection of dignity in the digital age. Article 12 of the UDHR states that "No one shall be subjected to arbitrary interference with his privacy, family, home or correspondence, nor to attacks upon his honour and reputation.

Everyone has the right to the protection of the law against such interference or attacks." Article 19 further says "Everyone has the right to freedom of opinion and expression; this right includes freedom to hold opinions without interference and to seek, receive and impart information and ideas through any media and regardless of frontiers.

New technology offers opportunities both to expand and to limit the freedom to communicate and the opportunity to protect private life. For example, new digital networks can provide a high level of security and privacy through the incorporation of such techniques as encryption. The Secure Socket Layer in Internet browser software enables the secure transfer of credit card numbers and reduces the risk that "sniffer" programs will capture credit card numbers. But encryption is not widely used for personal email. As a result it is relatively easy to capture private messages sent over the Internet.

New technology can also enable anonymous transactions over the Internet so that individuals can obtain access to information and purchase products without disclosing actual identity.

Some object to online anonymity and say that it could be a cloak for criminal conduct. But the question could fairly be asked why individuals should be required to disclose identity when such requirements did not exist in traditional information environments, such as the print world of newspapers and books or the broadcast world or radio and television.

Similar questions arise with the protocols for electronic mail services. Strong encryption products could ensure that individuals could exchange private messages with little concern that third parties would gain access to private messages. But slight modifications in these protocols, though such methods as "key escrow" or "key recovery" could enable the routine interception of personal communications.

Filtering techniques incorporated in the architecture of the Internet also raise far-reaching questions about the character and impact of the new communication services. These programs allow government and private enterprises to restrict access to information that is otherwise available Such methods could limit access to a wide range of important cultural, medical, and scientific information. Already these techniques have been used to limit access to public information.

Just as these new technologies are emerging that could significantly influence the future of human dignity on the digital age, technical organizations are playing an increasingly significant role in the policy world. Simultaneously, international organizations are playing an increasingly important role in shaping the policies for the Internet.

Main Challenges

New technology has always presented opportunities and risks. Industrialization promoted productivity and increased the standard of living in many parts of the world. Industrialization also caused enormous damage to the physical environment. Information technology also presents opportunity and risk. But the main challenges to human dignity in the digital age is not in the nature of the technology itself but in the capacity of individuals acting through democratic institutions to respond effectively to these new challenges.

These new challenges include the commercialization of the Internet, the growth of law enforcement authority, and the globalization of decision-making authority. There is also a critical need to understand the appropriate relationship between the two central interests of privacy and free expression.

The Commercialization of the Internet

Since the development of the World Wide Web in 1993, the character of the Internet has changed. The graphical interface has made it easier for many organizations to take advantage of global computer networks, to establish an online presence and to exchange information and ideas in the digital world. Educational institutions, cultural associations, scientific societies and others have all benefited from the dramatic growth of network communications. The web has also made possible the rapid development of new commercial applications that include both business to business services and business to consumer services.

Commercialization of the Internet also poses the threat that rights which would otherwise be protected in the political sphere will be turned over to the marketplace and individuals will be forced to pay for services that might otherwise be routinely provided. A critical example is the confidentiality of correspondence. By tradition, communication services have assured the privacy of personal correspondence and personal communication. But commercial forces have found that the records of communications and the transactions generated in the interactive environment are valuable for marketing purposes. Moreover, in the absence of legislation clearly establishing the privacy of new electronic communications, service providers may choose to offers communication services without assurance of confidentiality.

Citizens may then be required to purchase confidentiality for routine personal communication or to forgo privacy for commercial benefit. Two classes of Internet users may emerge: the "privacy haves" and the "privacy have-nots." Inherent in the provision of new communications services should be that confidentiality will be protected in law.

Commercialization of the Internet may pose a different challenge to freedom of expression. Here the concern is that market concentration and the consolidation of commercial power could transform the decentralized character of the Internet and reduce the number of voices and the opportunities for non-commercial speakers to participate in the Digital Age, It is therefore appropriate to ensure

There is a third challenge to the principles of Article 12 and 19 brought about by commercialization and that is the prospect that new techniques to track the use of copyright works in the digital environment, Copyright Management Systems, will be used to track the interests of Internet users. Such systems should be developed so as to permit compensation of copyright holders without the compelled disclosure of the identity of Internet users. In this context, anonymity protects both privacy and free expression.

The Growth of Law Enforcement Authority

Concerns about "cyber crime" and child pornography on the Internet have led to increased calls for government regulation and police investigation of the Internet. While there is a clear need to protect public safety and investigate and prosecute criminal wrongdoing it is vitally important that public concerns not lead to expansive new police powers that diminish procedural rights established in national law. Unrestricted government authority or government authority coupled with too little public accountability poses threats to the rights and freedoms of citizens in the age of the Internet.

For example, the Council of Europe has urged the adoption of a new convention on Cyber Crime. According to the Global Internet Liberty Campaign the proposal "is contrary to well established norms for the protection of the individual, that it improperly extends the police authority of national governments, that it will undermine the development of network security techniques, and that it will reduce government accountability in future law enforcement conduct."

Globalization of decisionmaking

The growth of the Internet has encouraged the rise of electronic commerce and the expansion of the global economy. As a consequence, international organizations, such as the World Trade Organization and the World Intellectual Property Organization have gained greater prominence in setting public policy for the digital age.

These developments pose specific challenges to human dignity, as these international organizations tend to emphasize commercial interests and do not generally recognize the broader values of cultural, social, political, or artistic activities, Individuals may also face the specific threat that rights accorded under national law may not be recognized by these international organizations.

To date most of the objection to globalization have focused on concerns about environmental protection and labor standards. But it may soon be the case that similar objections will be made when decisions concerning privacy and free expression are made by international organizations.

The Complimentary Roles of Privacy and Free Expression in the Digital Age

The final challenge to the protection of human dignity, and in particular privacy and free expression, is to understand that these two interests are complimentary and should be pursued jointly particularly as issues considering the design of new information technologies and new network architectures are considered.

Consider for example the question of whether web sites should routinely collect information about Internet users. This practice is at odds with both the protection of privacy and the promotion of free expression. Better practices will promote anonymity and enable individuals to receive information and ideas without the requirement of routine tracking and surveillance.

Therefore it is a mistake to argue for a "balance" of privacy and free expression. Both interests should be protection in the Digital Age. Free expression is not possible without the protection of private life.

In response to the challenges above, it is necessary to reaffirm support for the UDHR, promote Fair Information Practices and genuine Privacy Enhancing Technologies, remove barriers to the free flow of information, and strengthen public voice NGOs.

Reaffirm support for UDHR

It is critically important that the fundamental human rights articulated at the end of the second world war and the beginning of the age of computers are not lost as a result of rapid developments in technologies, the commercialization of the Internet, or the increase of globalization. Efforts should be made to promote public awareness of Article 12 and Article 19 and specific research on the application of these two key principles to communications and the digital age should be pursued.

International educational efforts to promote understanding and awareness of the UDHR and particularly Articles 12 and 19 should continue even though the fiftieth anniversary was recently celebrated. Significant decisions concerning the rights of privacy and free expression will be made by governments in the next few years.

Promote Fair Information Practices and genuine Privacy Enhancing Technologies

In the area of privacy protection, the primary goal should be to ensure adoption and enforcement of "Fair Information Practices" that are the basis for privacy protection around these world. These principles of data collection appropriately place obligations on organizations that collect personal information and grant rights to citizens and consumers who become the subjects or automated records and profiles. Fair Information practices

The United States and Europe have recently taken steps to adopt a "Safe Harbor." It remains to be seen whether this is an effective means to protest privacy where trans-border data flows occur. Consumer organizations have urged the development and adoption of an international convention on privacy as a more appropriate method to safeguard the interests of citizens.

It is also appropriate to encourage adoption of "Privacy Enhancing Technologies," but it is critical to assess these techniques to determine whether in fact they protect the interests of the citizen in the digital age. Encryption can be used both to protect the privacy of personal communication and to compel the disclosure of identity. Research should go forward on techniques that minimize or eliminate the collection of personally identifiable information but still allow for secure and verifiable transactions in the digital age. Such "clean" information technologies are critical to the design of networks that promote privacy and not surveillance.

It is also important to address the concern of unlawful police surveillance that takes place around the globe. The right of journalists, human rights organizers, and political surveillance should be protected against unlawful intrusions into private life. Efforts to report on the state of privacy, such as the annual report of Privacy International, should continue.

Remove Barriers to the Free Flow of Information and Preserve the Openness of the Internet

Efforts should go forward in the policy, commercial, and standard-setting realm to promote the free exchange of information and to maintain the openness of the Internet. The Internet continues to offer extraordinary opportunities to expand human knowledge, to strengthen human understanding, and to promote cooperation across borders. It is vitally important for civil society to encourage the continued exchange of information and ideas made possible by the new communications technology.

Efforts by government to restrict access to information on the Internet or to limit the distribution of information on the Internet, particularly information that is political, cultural or artistic should be opposed.

Standard-setting organization should promote open, non-proprietary standards that enable competition and discourage the development of "bottlenecks" in the communications infrastructure. These organizations should also discourage the adoption of network-based techniques that "filter" information, which is more accurately described as "digital censorship." While individual users may choose to use software that limits access to certain information, the use of these techniques at the network level is a direct threat to freedom of expression in the digital world.

Strengthen Public Voice NGOs

Central to the protection of human dignity in the digital age is the active participation of civil society organizations in decisions concerning the future of the Internet. Fortunately, the growth of the Internet has also witnessed the growth of a new type of Non Governmental Organizations (NGOs). These NGOs are easily identified by their ".org" suffix. They are independent of the government (.gov) and business organizations (.com). They focus on the social issues arising from the impact of information technology, such as privacy and free expression, but they also use the Internet for public education, organizing, and public action. Typically, they maintain a web site, publish an electronic newsletter, organize public campaigns, issue reports, and host conferences.

The organizations are involved in decisions made by national government, international organizations, such as the OECD, the UN, and the European Union, as well as technical standards bodies, such as the IETF and the W3C. The organizations bring a "public voice" (civil society) perspective to emerging digital age issues based on international human rights norms, such as the Universal Declaration of Human Rights. Although the groups are relatively small and informal, they are already having a significant impact on Internet policy.

Their work should be encouraged. Governments engaged in Internet policy, particularly at the international level, must ensure that the "Public Voice" is sufficiently represented in all decision-making activities. Successful policies for the Internet must include the voices of consumers and citizens.

To safeguard the rights of privacy and freedom of expression in the digital age, it is necessary to reaffirm support for the Universal Declaration of Human Rights, particularly Article 12 and Article 19; promote the implementation of "Fair Information Practices" and the development of genuine Privacy Enhancing Technologies; remove barriers to the free flow of information; and encourage the participation of "Public Voice" NGOs in decisions concerning the future of the Internet society.

2

Meaning and Sources of Human Rights

The Second World War saw "civilized" nations commit atrocities against their own and other populations on an unprecedented scale. One of the most significant responses to the abuses which occurred was the agreement among nations which came to be known as the Universal Declaration of Human Rights. Since the Declaration was made in 1948 there have been many new international covenants and treaties and the development of a body of international and domestic human rights law. "Bills of Rights" and "human rights" are closely related concepts, and in Australia they have become part of a linked debate. The most notable outcome of this local debate is a continuing lack of support for a Bill of Rights politically, arguably based upon a perceived opposition to implementation of "human rights" in the wider community.

Part of the difficulty in the debate is the gulf between the understanding of human rights by advocates of a Bill of Rights and many, though not all, of those who oppose a Bill. The Committee has received a number of detailed submissions which, for instance, describe human rights as if they are in opposition to protections given under the common law. Other writers of submissions appeared not to be aware that rights "protected" under common law can be overridden by legislation by either State or Federal governments.

This chapter outlines some of the definitions of "human rights" presented during the inquiry, and examines the source of human rights.

The Meaning of "Human Rights"

The Committee recognises that the concept of human rights has cultural, moral, religious and social dimensions and a theoretical background that goes back at least as far as the writings of political philosophers such as John Locke in the 17 th century. In the rest of this chapter the committee approaches human rights from a legal and political perspective, but it is important to briefly outline what is understood by the term "human rights".

Human rights are those rights that are universal across all nations. They are based upon the belief that each individual should be treated with the dignity and respect to which, as a human being, they are entitled. One way to define "human rights" then, is that they are part of what each person needs to be human. Human rights, defined in conventions and legislation, are an attempt to express how people's humanity should be respected by those with power over them, particularly governments. The United Nations Declaration on Human Rights encapsulates this in its first two articles:

— All human beings are born free and equal in dignity and rights. They are endowed with reason and conscience and should act towards one another in a spirit of brotherhood.

— Everyone is entitled to all the rights and freedoms set forth in this Declaration, without distinction of any kind, such as race, colour, sex, language, religion, political or other opinion, national or social origin, property, birth or other status.

These rights are given expression in different forms in the various humans rights declarations, treaties and covenants,. Thus there are :

- 'civil and political rights' – such as rights to life, liberty, free speech, movement, political thought and religious practice, a fair trial, privacy, to found a family and to vote;
- 'economic, social and cultural rights' – such as rights to adequate food and water, health care, education, a clean environment, to respect for cultural practices, and to welfare assistance;
- humanitarian rights – that is the rights of those who are involved in, or affected by, armed conflict, such as the treatment of prisoners of war, of the wounded or sick or shipwrecked, of civilians, and of women and children in particular;
- various categories of rights as defined by the nature of the holders – such as the rights of workers, women, children, minority groups, refugees, indigenous peoples, and people with a disability.

In some of the evidence to this inquiry quoted in later chapters there is reference to "generations" in the development of human rights. "First Generation rights" are those from the immediate post war period, exemplified by the Declaration and the International Covenant on Civil and Political Rights (ICCPR). These rights are particularly focussed on restraining the state from committing abuses on its citizens of the type witnessed during the 1930s and 40s. Typically, "First Generation" rights are expressed as individual civil and political rights, and are those most familiar to Western democracies. "Second Generation rights" are economic, social and cultural rights, as exemplified by the *International Covenant of Economic Social and Cultural Rights (ICESCR).* The rights are primarily concerned with matters such as housing, clothing, food, education and social security, which the individual or group requires to enjoy these rights fully. "Third Generation rights" in contrast derived from developing countries and those with Socialist governments, who saw the rights of "groups" as being overlooked by the traditional focus on individual liberties.

Limits on Human Rights

Human Rights, despite being universal, have limits. Rights such as the right to be free from torture or slavery, are generally considered to be absolute, but most other rights have been subject to qualification or limitation in some way. The most important limits on human rights are:

- The generality with which rights are expressed in conventions
- Limitation clauses within individual rights; and
- Limits caused by competing rights

The generality of the expression of rights is a product of how they have developed and how they are agreed upon. The so-called "first generation" human rights were heavily influenced by liberal political philosophy with its emphasis on the individual and their rights against the state. The formulation of the rights owed much to both the Common Law in English-speaking countries and the Civil Law system applying in European countries. However human rights have come to encompass other influences, particularly with the so-called second and third generation rights. The concepts embodied in current human rights documents come from many different traditions, countries and cultures. Religious systems such as Christianity, Judaism and Islam have also influenced the concepts behind human rights, while more recent movements such as feminism, socialism and environmentalism have also influenced rights and conventions. Many of these influences have conflicting values and there is no agreed way to resolve these so as to identify a "human right" other than the process of negotiation which exists between countries in the development of conventions, declarations and treaties.

Because human rights have different contexts in different cultures, yet are at the same time universal, they are of necessity written in very general language. This allows nations to interpret those rights within their own cultural context. As Justice Brennan of the High Court has said:

An attempt to define human rights and fundamental freedoms exhaustively is bound to fail, for the respective religious, cultural and political systems of the world would attribute differing contents to the notions of freedom and dignity and would perceive at least some difference in the rights and freedoms that are conducive to their attainment.

The formulation of many rights also contain limitation clauses. This was explained by one witness to the inquiry:

For example, if we take article 19 and 19(3) of the International Covenant on Civil and Political Rights, we will see that the limitation on the right to free speech is cast in the following terms: it says that the right itself carries special duties and responsibilities. The covenant accepts that the right to free speech is not absolute.

The covenant then says that the right may be limited where the limitation or restriction is provided by law and is necessary in a democratic society. It sets out the reasons or grounds on which the limitation will apply. The first ground is the rights and reputations of others. It goes on to list other grounds such as national security, public morals and public order.

An example such as this illustrates that most rights are not absolute. Another limitation on rights is that typically one right has to be balanced against another. An example of the balancing of the right to freedom of religion as against the right for women not to be discriminated against was explored in a Committee hearing in relation to the ordination of women priests:

The answer comes from the definition of the rights themselves. At this stage we have only the international covenants to work from. Article 18.1 of the International Covenant on Civil and Political Rights protects that religion in its current form so that the current teachings, practices, observance and worship of that religion are protected by a right of religion. What is protected is the freedom to exercise one's religious beliefs. We would then be seeing a conflict with a right for all people to be treated equally. The right to equality is not an absolute right. The balance would have to be struck between two sets of competing rights and the covenants make it very clear that one person's rights may well be limited by the enjoyment and exercise of another right. In some senses, even if churches were brought within the scheme of the bill of rights, it would be to protect the churches, to protect current forms of religious organisations so that they are the beneficiaries of the rights themselves. If there is a conflict between the nature of the enjoyment of a particular religious belief and the rights of another, then the process is finding where that balance is to be struck.

While most human rights are not absolute, at least in their expression in conventions and treaties, they can be described as interdependent and indivisible. Countries that have signed the

ICCPR for instance, have agreed to protect all of the rights contained in that instrument. This goes back to human rights being those rights which express how people's humanity should be respected: governments cannot pick and choose which aspects of being human they will respect.

Rights and Responsibilities

A debate in the human rights area, and one which forms the term of reference (c) of this inquiry, is to what extent "responsibilities" should be included when human rights are expressed in conventions and in local legislation. Every right implies a responsibility on the member state to honour that right. When the 1948 Declaration was drafted the strongest concern was to protect individual rights against the state, after the recent experience of authoritarian governments before and during the War. Governments were given responsibilities to protect their citizens' rights. However there have been arguments in recent years that part of being a citizen involves accepting responsibilities, and that over-emphasis on rights creates an attitude of avoidance of individual responsibility. This debate will be covered in later chapters. The Committee notes here that many international covenants do discuss responsibilities alongside rights, and that recently a Universal Declaration of Responsibilities has been drafted by an international non-government organisation.

Major International Covenants

While the meaning of human rights is the subject of some debate, the sources of current human rights law is generally accepted. The original source document for current human rights is the United Nations Declaration of Human Rights, adopted in 1948 by the majority of the international community in response to the abuses of human rights perpetrated before and during the Second World War. It expresses basic human rights in general terms as a common standard of achievement for all peoples and all nations. These rights include the prevention of slavery and torture, the right to be treated equally regardless of race or gender, the right to own property and the right to privacy.

The covenant which has proved most influential in the development of human rights law has been the International Covenant on Civil and Political Rights (the ICCPR). This was adopted in 1966 to provide detailed explanation of the individual rights of the citizen in relation to the power of the state. Civil and political rights include the right to vote, the right to form trade unions, the right not to suffer cruel or unusual punishment and various protections to ensure a person is not subject to arbitrary arrest or detention without charge. Under Article 40 those states, such as Australia, which have ratified the Convention are given obligations to provide reports on progress in implementing the protection of these rights within their jurisdictions.

In the international community there was debate, led by developing nations, as to whether the individual rights protected by the ICCPR gave sufficient recognition to the problems faced in countries where inadequate food, housing and health resources were the primary consideration of its citizens. There was also a debate along ideological lines with Socialist countries arguing that rights such as those relating to employment or welfare were not properly encompassed in the ICCPR. The idea of broader rights to be enjoyed by groups and individuals, drawing from the economic, social and cultural rights discussed in the 1948 Declaration, then became enshrined in the International Covenant on Economic, Social and Cultural Rights (ICESCR), also adopted in 1966. The

ICESCR provides for the right to be free from hunger, the right to education, the right to social security, the right to physical and mental health and the right of groups to enjoy their own culture and participate in cultural life. As with the ICCPR, those countries, such as Australia, that have ratified the ICESCR have obligations to report on progress in implementing the Convention in their jurisdictions. However, while the ICCPR is prescriptive in the obligations imposed, the ICESCR's obligations are aspirational in nature.

There are many other international treaties and conventions to which Australia is a signatory. Some of these are largely commercial or trade agreements whereas others concern social factors. Apart from the Declaration and the ICCPR, some of the conventions which have had an influence on the development of Australian law include:

- The Convention on the Rights of the Child
- The International Convention on the Elimination of Racial Discrimination
- The Convention Relating to the Status of Refugees
- United Nations Draft Declaration on the rights of Indigenous Peoples; and
- The Convention on the Elimination of all forms of Discrimination Against Women.

Two points need to be made in relation to these international agreements. Firstly, regardless of whether NSW has a Bill of Rights these international agreements have and will continue to have an influence on NSW through their impact on both Federal and State legislation and through their impact on the common law. Secondly, a local Bill of Rights does not need to adopt the terms of some or all of these conventions. The Declaration and these conventions form what is often termed as "the International Bill of Rights". These international instruments are the core of human rights law that can be adapted or expressed in terms relevant to local conditions in a Bill of Rights.

Human Rights Protection in NSW

When the Queensland Legal Constitutional and Administrative Committee considered a Bill of Rights one of the outcomes of its inquiry was a study it commissioned into the rights protected under existing Queensland law. In this inquiry the committee found the submissions from Australian Lawyers for Human Rights and the Law Society of New South Wales particularly helpful because they began with an examination of the "rights" currently protected in New South Wales. These cover the following areas:

- Protections under the Constitution
- Protections in Federal legislation
- Protections in NSW legislation
- Common Law protections, and
- International remedies.

Protections under the Constitution

The Commonwealth Constitution contains several rights, mainly expressed as prohibitions on Federal or State powers. These are limited and ad hoc rather than forming a coherent collection of specific rights. However these rights cannot be overruled by any statute passed by any Parliament in Australia. Section 116, prohibiting the Commonwealth from making laws with respect to the establishment of, or prohibition on the exercise of religion, is perhaps the best known. Other rights include:

- Under s 51(xxxi) the Commonwealth may only compulsorily acquire property if it does so on just terms (ie with compensation)
- Section 80 provides the right to trial by jury for federal indictable offences
- Section 117 protects residents from one state from special disability or discrimination based upon residence, in other states, and
- The separation of powers contained in Chapter Three of the Constitution, which establishes the High Court, also provides some protection from inappropriate use of executive power.

A further protection is provided by s109 of the Constitution which renders State legislation invalid where it is inconsistent with Federal legislation. The width of the Federal anti-discrimination statutes means that there is significant scope for Federal legislation to protect human rights against action by States and territories. However s109 can also be used by a Federal government to override State legislation which protects rights.

The High Court in recent years has also found "implied rights" in the Constitution. For example, using sections 7 and 24, the High Court found an implied right to freedom of political communications, overturning limits placed upon political adverting on radio and television during an election campaign . This implied right was also developed in relation to defamation of politicians in the Theophanous case.

Protection of Rights in Federal Legislation

Some significant rights are given to particular groups in NSW under either Federal or State legislation. The basis for much of this is the anti-discrimination statutes, most of which date from the mid 1970s to the early 80s. Federal governments have passed legislation protecting different categories of persons from discrimination which draw upon principles from the ICCPR and covenants addressing discrimination issues. This legislation includes the Sex Discrimination Act 1984, the Disability Discrimination Act 1992 and the Racial Discrimination Act 1975.

Under the Human Rights and Equal Opportunity Commission Act 1986 the Human Rights and Equal Opportunity Commission (HREOC) was established to oversee the protection of these rights.

The Commission was given investigatory and reporting powers but, following the case of Brandy v Human Rights and Equal Opportunity Commission, HREOC is not able to provide enforceable legal remedies. Included in schedule 2 of the 1986 Act is the ICCPR, as breaches of human rights by Commonwealth agencies are defined by that instrument.

There are other Federal statutes which provide direct or indirect protection of what are commonly regarded as human rights. These include:

- The Privacy Act 1988 (Cth), which guarantees the rights to privacy contained in article 17 of the ICCPR
- The Freedom of Information Act 1982 (Cth) which gives limited rights to obtain personal information held by Federal agencies
- The Evidence Act 1995 (Cth) which gives judges a discretion to exclude improperly or illegally obtained evidence
- The Family Law Act 1975 (Cth) which has incorporated principles from the Convention on the Rights of the Child.

Protections of Rights in NSW Legislation

The protections given under NSW statutes follow the same pattern of protecting rights based upon principles established in international instruments for a limited number of categories of groups or individuals. The key act is the Anti-Discrimination Act 1977, with an Anti Discrimination Board to oversee its implementation. The Disability Services Act 1993 sets out a range of non-enforceable principles relating to the treatment of people with disabilities. Privacy and related protections are also included to a limited extent in the Privacy and Personal Information Protection Act 1998 (NSW) and the Freedom of Information Act 1989 (NSW) although these only address rights against State government agencies

Common Law protections

The common law over the centuries since Magna Carta, and particularly since the Bill of Rights Act 1689 (UK) has developed a series of protections of individual liberties and due process. These are primarily "left over" rights – the Federal and NSW Parliaments are at all times free to pass legislation which abrogates these rights, and only those common law protections which are not limited by statute remain in force. Despite this, common law rights have had a major and continuing impact on criminal law and related areas. They include the right against self incrimination, the right (under tort law) to sue for false imprisonment, and the immunity from search without a warrant. Other important protections include the presumption of the onus of proof being on the prosecution to prove a criminal offence; and the requirement that the standard of proof in criminal cases is that of proven beyond reasonable doubt. Each of these rights can be, and sometimes are, overruled by statute, and their application is also largely dependent upon the discretion of individual judges. The writ of habeas corpus, however, by which an individual can seek redress for false imprisonment, is still very much able to be used in the protection of human rights.

Aside from the "traditional" common law rights there is the potential for further protections via rules of statutory interpretation. Under common law rules of statutory interpretation, judges can use international human rights instruments to assist them in interpreting statutes or the common law. Justice Kirby of the High Court has explained this approach:

In judging whether a right is fundamental, regard might be had to any relevant constitutional or statutory provisions and to the common law.... It is also helpful, in considering fundamental rights, to take cognisance of international statements of such rights, appearing in instruments to which Australia is a party, particularly where breach of such rights give rise to procedures of individual complaint. These provisions reflect notions with which Australian law is generally compatible. To the fullest extent possible, save where statute or established common law authority is clearly inconsistent with such rights, the common law in Australia, when it is being developed or re-expressed, should be formulated in a way that is compatible with such international and universal jurisprudence.

As well as interpretation, judges can also use international law to develop new rights in the common law. A very important case in this regard was Minister for Immigration and Ethnic Affairs v Teoh. In this case the High Court ruled that, as the Commonwealth had ratified the Convention on the Rights of the Child, the decision-maker had to give consideration to the rights in that Convention when considering how to protect the applicants interests, even though the

Convention had not been implemented by domestic legislation. Another example of the influence of international human rights on domestic common law is the found in the Dietrich case, 32 where it was deemed that a litigant who was unable to obtain legal representation had been denied the common law right to fair trial.

International Remedies

Under certain circumstances, an individual may seek an international remedy from one of the three main international committees that receive complaints. These committees are the Human Rights Committee, established under the ICCPR; the Committee on the Convention for the Elimination of All Forms of Racial Discrimination; and the Torture Committee established under the Convention against Torture. Any findings by a committee that human rights are violated, and any recommendations to address this, are not binding on Federal or State governments, although action is sometimes taken to avoid adverse international opinion. An example where a successful complaint to the Human Rights Committee resulted in remedial action by the Federal government was a complaint in the 1990s against provisions in the criminal law in Tasmania, which made certain types of homosexual activity by consenting adults an indictable offence. Following an adverse finding by the Human Rights Committee, the Federal government passed the Human Rights (Sexual Conduct) Act 1994 (Cth), which overrode the Tasmanian law.

The Adequacy of Current Protections

The description of current protections of human rights above is provided as a context for the debate on the need for a Bill of

Rights, discussed in Chapters Five and Six; it is not intended in this Chapter to argue that humans right are or are not adequately protected under existing laws. Those who support a Bill of Rights believe these current protections in New South Wales are ad hoc, narrowly focussed and inadequate. They see a Bill of Rights as necessary to provide a comprehensive framework for the protection of rights.

Those who oppose a Bill of Rights believe the essential protections necessary to prevent human rights abuses already exist, in current laws, and, more importantly, through the institutions of responsible and democratic government and an independent judiciary. They argue that it is the current constitutional structure which has prevented (or limited) human rights abuses, and that a Bill of Rights would undermine the stability of the structure.

3

The Nature of Human Rights

The concept of human rights arises, a concept which tends to emphasise the worth of the individual and to recognise his or her rights as against their society. As generally used today, the term "human rights" covers the series of often disparate rights and freedoms asserted by many to be universally accepted and essential prerequisites for peoples' enjoyment of a life based on the centrality of human dignity.

Proponents of human rights regard them as being inherent, inalienable and universal: inherent in the sense that they are the birthright of all human beings, in that people enjoy these rights simply by reason of their humanity and, as such, they do not have to be granted or bestowed by a Sovereign for them to be enjoyed; inalienable, in the sense that people cannot agree to give them up or have them taken away from them; and universal in that they do not just apply to "men", or "citizens" or "ethnic minorities", but to all persons, regardless of their nationality, status, sex or race.

From a contemporary international law perspective, the concept of human rights can more precisely be defined as those fundamental rights and freedoms incorporated into the body of international law, by having been acknowledged by states (in theory if not always in practice and whether by custom or by binding treaty) as being universal in nature.

Recognition of essential needs such as freedom and dignity is implicit in some of the earliest written codes from ancient Babylon, which refer to the need to help the poor and dispossessed; in Hindu and Buddhist texts which focus on the human condition;.in notions of human virtue and compassion which characterise early Confucianism; and in the natural law tradition of the West. Throughout all, there is recognition that, in human relations, some principles will always hold and that some common standards of behaviour can be regarded as universally valid.

An historical examination of human rights theory and practice will illustrate the various dimensions to the concept of human rights. Given the historical origins of human rights, much of this will focus on Western experience. This does not imply that the concept of human rights is not relevant to non-Western views of human dignity. Since 1945, the concept of human rights has increasingly become universally recognised as a basic tenet of international law and a legitimate subject for discussion between states.

Much of this is due to the crucial and pioneering role which the United Nations has played in fostering and promoting the philosophy and practice of human rights among its member states. However, the seminal notion that human beings are endowed - purely by reason of their humanity - with certain fundamental and inalienable rights, benefits and protections, is an idea which has existed to various degrees in all societies.

In the context of Western political philosophy, it was the emphasis which classical Greek philosophy placed on an examination of the individual, in particular the individual's role in the running of a civil society - the "polis" - which became a precursor to the philosophical debate on the "Rights of Man"; a debate which has continued ever since throughout the history of the West. Even during the time of Plato and Socrates, this issue was linked to the kindred notions of Natural Law and Idealism. On the basis of these ideas it was later argued that, above and beyond the real world of the laws and rules promulgated by kings and emperors (the so-called "positive law"), there existed certain immutable and "natural" laws to which all humanity is entitled and by which all rulers should be judged. Such views were taken up and developed by the Stoics and later Christian thinkers such as St Augustine.

In later centuries, the struggle between the prerogatives of the Crown and the rights of the subjects led to the development of fundamental civil rights. In England, for example, these rights were first protected in 1215 by the Magna Carta as well as by the Common Law principles of due process and the writ of habeas corpus. Such ideas were eventually given clear expression in the 1689 Bill of Rights, with which the English philosopher Locke was closely associated.

It was the second half of the Eighteenth Century, however - in particular the Age of Enlightenment - which witnessed a major development in the commitment of European societies to the concept of human rights. Building on political concepts such as the "law of nations" propounded by the Dutch jurist Grotius to demonstrate the secularisation of natural law, the "social contract" of Rousseau, Montesquieu's concept of the "separation of powers", as well as the writings of Locke, proponents of the theory of the "rights of man" fought to have these philosophical ideas reflected and protected in their societies at the practical and concrete level. This movement in turn would, in the late 1700s, have revolutionary consequences for both the French monarchy and the British colonies of North America.

What was most significant about this particular period of the history of Western political philosophy was that ideas about the rights of man led to the promulgation of rules which were incorporated into the constituent documents of newly emerged revolutionary states. In the American Declaration of Independence of 1776, one finds the famous lines:

> *....we take these truths to be self-evident, that all men are created equal, and that they are endowed by their Creator with certain unalienable Rights, that among these are Life, Liberty and the pursuit of Happiness.*

Likewise, Article 1 of the France's 1789 Declaration of the Rights of Man and the Citizen echoes these sentiments when it states that

> *all men are born and remain free and equal in their rights.*

Both the 1776 American and the 1789 French Declarations represent important steps in the historical evolution of thinking about human rights, as they reflect systematic attempts to enshrine human rights as fundamental constituent and guiding principles for newly emerged nations. These aspirations, inspired to a large extent by the experience of individuals' struggle against arbitrary rule, sought to offer citizens "fundamental freedoms", that is, basic guarantees against the arbitrary exercise of power by their state.

It is of note that the modern interest in human rights throughout the world and its concomitant description as a universal concept has tended to develop at a time when states and rulers in all regions have demonstrated their increased power to control or otherwise unilaterally affect the lives of individuals. It can be argued that the proliferation of the "modern state" has also led to the parallel growth of human rights and that, the universality of human rights is a clear reaction to the universalisation of the "modern state" as the dominant form of political and social organisation.

These notions of the rights of man as expounded at this time were far from universal: they only applied to the citizens of such states as were willing to proclaim and observe these rights on behalf of their citizens. They were hardly regarded as applying to all members of humanity - in particular, to slaves, prisoners of war or stateless persons. This was because the principal tenet of international intercourse -national sovereignty - reigned supreme, as did the related assumption that states (or the Sovereign) could treat their citizens or subjects as they wished, without any fear of outside interference.

There are several instances, however, where states directly raised "human rights" concerns with other Sovereigns in terms which could have been regarded as interference in the sovereignty of that state. For example, in 1744, the British and Dutch successfully interceded on behalf of Prague's Jewish community threatened with deportation by the authorities of Bohemia.

In the eighteenth and nineteenth centuries, political frictions concerning the rights of Christian minorities were another factor in developing and extending the concept of human rights.

An alternative to Great Power intervention to protect these minorities was the use of international treaties expressly providing for their protection: one of the earliest examples of this was the Treaty of Kucuk-Kainardji (1774) whereby the Ottoman Empire undertook to protect Christians in their territories, including by granting the Russian Tsar the right to make representations on their behalf. This was followed in 1878 by the Treaty of Berlin, which expressly allowed third states to make representations on behalf of these Christian minorities.

In addition, the efforts of the Abolitionists in securing a ban on the slave trade and the abolition of the institution of slavery in the nineteenth century, first at the 1815 Congress of Vienna, then at the Brussels Congress of the 1880s and finally by means of the 1926 Slavery Convention, also need to be recalled. These were important historical milestones in securing the practical application of the basic human rights principle of human equality.

A related development occurred in the field of the laws regulating the protection of persons in time of war, so-called "international humanitarian law". The establishment of the International Committee of the Red Cross (ICRC) and the entry into force of the 1864 Geneva Convention were crucial events which would have clear repercussions for the development of human rights.

With the establishment of the League of Nations after the First World War, human rights were further developed in the international sphere: while human rights were not expressly mentioned in the Covenant of the League of Nations, the organisation was active in seeking to protect the rights of peoples in two particular spheres, namely the protection of minorities and of persons inhabiting the colonies of the defeated powers. The former manifested itself in the requirement that admission to the League of new states with ethnic minorities was often preconditioned upon their being required to enter into minority protection treaties or other similar guarantees.

These minorities rights were in turn enforceable by the members of the League. Similarly, the need to protect the inhabitants of colonies led to the creation of the League's Mandate system, which was guided by the overriding principle that "the well being and development of such peoples form a sacred trust of civilization". Australia was one of the League members to be granted mandates over former enemy colonies, in the former German colonies of New Guinea and Nauru.

Another important field from the human rights perspective in which the League was active was in the protection of workers' rights, and indeed the goal of "fair and humane conditions of labour for men, women and children" was expressly mentioned in the League's Covenant. This particular objective was put into practice through the International Labour Organisation (ILO) which was established in 1919. The ILO has since been instrumental in promoting and monitoring compliance with international labour standards.

The horrors of the Second World War led to the birth and recognition of the modern human rights movement as a cornerstone of the new post-war international order..President Roosevelt's proclamation in 1941 of the Four Freedoms (that is, of speech and expression, of belief, freedom from fear, and freedom from want) as a universally applicable set of standards established, along with the work of non-governmental organisations, the groundwork for this movement. But it was the establishment of the United Nations in 1945 and the provisions of the UN Charter which ushered in a new period of international concern for, and commitment to, human rights. In the second preambular paragraph of the UN Charter, this commitment is reflected in Members' determination -

> *to reaffirm faith in fundamental human rights, in the dignity and worth of the human person, in the equal rights of men and women and of nations large and small....*

A major shift in the thinking behind the UN Charter, as compared to the League, was its emphasis on the universal rights of all people, not just specific groups such as minorities or colonial inhabitants. For example, Article 1 of the UN Charter sets out the purposes of the UN and included in these are:

> 1(2)To develop friendly relations among nations based on respect for the principle of equal rights and self-determination of peoples, and to take other appropriate measures to strengthen universal peace.
>
> 1(3) To achieve international co-operation in solving international problems of an economic, social, cultural, or humanitarian character, and in promoting and encouraging respect for human rights and for fundamental freedoms for all without distinction as to race, sex, language or religion.

The implications of the notion that universally applicable standards of human rights exist as a matter of international law and practice, and which have to be observed by all governments, have been far-reaching: states could no longer hide behind the defence that abuse of human rights was an internal affair, since human rights were now firmly and progressively established as a matter of legitimate international concern.

A cornerstone of this post-war human rights regime is the Universal Declaration of Human Rights, adopted on 10 December 1948, later to be designated as "Human Rights Day". Although not a legally binding treaty, the Universal Declaration establishes an internationally recognised set of standards applicable to all persons without qualification. Its uniqueness lies in the fact that it represents a world-wide charter of rights, proclaiming as it does universal and fundamental freedoms which transcend national, religious, cultural and ideological factors. In this respect, it remains the most fundamental expression of international human rights standards.

The Universal Declaration is regarded as the basic cornerstone of the international human rights system and provides the foundation upon which the International Covenant on Civil and Political Rights (ICCPR), the International Covenant of Economic Social and Cultural Rights (ICESCR) and other international legal standards have been developed in relation to freedom from torture and racial discrimination, and the rights of women and children. The universality and continuing validity of the Universal Declaration were reaffirmed by the international.community in the 1993 Vienna Declaration and Programme of Action adopted by the Vienna World Conference on Human Rights, attended by 171 countries.

The role which the United Nations system has played in the post-war period in securing the promotion and protection of human rights cannot be over estimated. The United Nations has devoted considerable time, resources and effort to the promotion of human rights, both through its role in the drafting of human rights instruments and through the ongoing focus it places on human rights situations throughout the world.

Some parameters of contemporary human rights practice

It would be useful at this point to raise some of the key and, at times, controversial themes which invariably arise in the modern practice of human rights, both in order to clarify further the concept of human rights as well as to illustrate that human rights is a constantly developing field of international law and relations, and one which raises fundamental issues affecting many areas of international relations.

The rights proclaimed by the UDHR are often divided into two distinct thematic categories of rights: on the one hand, the so-called civil and political rights (Articles 1 to 21) as distinct from economic, social and cultural rights (Articles 22 to 28).

This conceptual dichotomy is reflected in the existence of two separate Covenants, the ICCPR and the ICESCR. These three instruments are often referred to as the International Bill of Human Rights.

Civil and political rights are those rights which historically have been regarded as the basic rights from which the whole philosophy of human rights developed, namely the protection of the individual from the arbitrary exercise of power by the state. These rights are often referred to as "first generation rights". A common claim made about these rights is that they are "negative" rights, in the sense that the state is required to refrain from certain actions against the individual, with the result that the individual can enjoy the freedom to be left alone to pursue, within acceptable limits, happiness and prosperity. This is a correct assertion in principle, but states often have to undertake many "positive" acts - such as training police and judiciaries, or establishing appropriate organs - in order to safeguard civil and political rights.

The class of civil rights is usually taken to include those rights set out in Articles 1 to 18 of the UDHR, incorporating "physical integrity rights" such as the right to life and the protection against torture, and "due process rights" such as the right to a fair trial, the presumption of innocence and the right to legal representation.

Political rights include freedom of expression, freedom of association and assembly and the right to vote in free and genuine elections by secret ballot.

Economic, social and cultural rights encapsulate those rights concerned with the material, social and cultural welfare of persons, and were originally set out in Articles 22 to 28 of the Universal Declaration. These rights are often described as "positive" or "distributive" rights, since they require an activist response by the state to ensure the provision of those social goods and services - such as housing,.clothing, food, education, or social security - conducive to the realisation and enjoyment of these rights by all persons. While these rights are often defined as "second generation" rights, this may be a misnomer since some of the first internationally recognised human rights (the Berne Convention and work of the ILO in particular) were in fact social ones.

In recent years, there have been various proponents of a "third generation" of human rights which have also been called "group" or "solidarity" rights. Examples of such rights include the right to peace and the right to the enjoyment of a healthy environment. However, it is far from clear that these have any established status in international law or that they can be considered as part of the current human rights regime. Indeed care should be taken when considering such principles, as, while they may be laudable objectives per se, they should not be seen as overtaking or displacing the universally accepted civil, political, economic, social and cultural rights.

The need for maintaining "quality control" when examining the viability and necessity of new instruments in the human rights field has been acknowledged by both independent commentators as well as by the UN itself. UN General Assembly resolution 41/120 of 4 December 1986 sets out various parameters to be considered when developing new human rights instruments, for example, the need to be consistent with the existing corpus of human rights instruments and the ability to ensure the effective implementation of the new instruments.

The universality and indivisibility of human rights

Ever since the UN Charter first recognised the fundamental nature of human rights in the international sphere, there has been a debate concerning the universality and indivisibility of human rights. Wide differences of view have existed regarding the nature and relevance of cultural, religious and other factors with respect to the practical observance of human rights. One view has been that human rights - in particular civil and political rights - are essentially Western constructs reflecting a Western world view, born out of European political history and colonialism.

The same criticism has often been addressed to international law in general. A corollary of this view has been resistance by developing countries to the imposition of human rights values on the basis that these rights are merely another manifestation of neo-colonialism and Western cultural imperialism, and accordingly do not adequately reflect, let alone acknowledge, non-Western value systems.

A variation of this argument has been to insist that the practical observance of human rights by each country should be undertaken in the context of its own particular culture and political system. This is an issue which (since the end of the Cold War) has assumed greater prominence.

The Australian approach to human rights takes as a basic premise that human rights are both universal and indivisible, and uses the terms of the UN Charter itself as its basic reference point. The UN Charter's Preamble is particularly relevant, as reference is made to Members' determination:.

> *to reaffirm faith in fundamental human rights, in the dignity and worth of the human person, in the equal rights of men and women and of nations large and small....*

The Charter expressly recognised that human rights were intended to be regarded as universal in application, that is, they were meant to apply to all countries, not merely Western countries. Similarly, the Universal Declaration was premised on this view of the applicability and scope of human rights. Similar observations apply to consideration of the later Covenants.

The view that the principles embodied in the Universal Declaration do not apply to those newly independent states which became UN Members in the 1960s and 1970s needs to be rejected. Not only does it ignore the fact that all new members of the UN agree to accept and carry out the obligations of the Charter upon joining the UN (and that Article 4 of the Charter expressly sets this out as a precondition to UN membership), but it also ignores the fact that the overwhelming majority of these states have endorsed the Universal Declaration and its underlying principles: for example, over 130 countries have ratified the two Covenants and indeed many of these countries have incorporated the Universal Declaration into their Constitutions. In addition, numerous UN resolutions have expressly reaffirmed the universality and indivisibility of all human rights, while the number of such resolutions which refer to the Universal Declaration is immense.

It should also be recalled that, at the first UN International Conference on Human Rights held in Tehran in 1968, more than eighty-five countries, the overwhelming majority of which were not Western, accepted, in paragraph 2 of the Proclamation of Tehran, the view that -

> *The Universal Declaration of Human Rights states a common understanding of the peoples of the world concerning the inalienable and inviolable rights of all members of the human family and constitutes an obligation for the members of the international community.*

A more recent reaffirmation of the universality of human rights was made twenty five years later at the 1993 Vienna World Conference of Human Rights. Paragraph 1 of the Vienna Declaration states that -

The World Conference on Human Rights reaffirms the solemn commitment of all States to fulfil their obligations to promote universal respect for, and observance and protection of, all human rights and fundamental freedoms for all in accordance with the Charter, other instruments relating to human rights, and international law. The universal nature of these rights and freedoms is beyond doubt.

Similarly, the Australian approach has been to reject the view that there exists a hierarchy or priority with respect to those rights embodied in the Universal Declaration.

In Australia's view, the Declaration does not rank or prioritise some rights above others or impose preconditions on the enjoyment of some of these rights. As far as Australia is concerned, all the rights in the Universal Declaration.are closely inter-related, interdependent and, above all, indivisible. To quote again from the Vienna Declaration:

All human rights are universal, indivisible and interdependent and interrelated. The international community must treat human rights globally in a fair and equal manner, on the same footing, and with the same emphasis.

While the significance of national and regional particularities and various historical, cultural and religious backgrounds must be borne in mind, it is the duty of States, regardless of their political, economic and cultural systems, to promote and protect all human rights and fundamental freedoms.

One result of this approach is the rejection of the view that conditions can be placed by governments on the observance of civil and political rights, on the basis that greater prominence should be given to addressing economic development problems.

Similarly, economic, social or cultural rights should not be accorded less priority than, or waived in favour of, political and civil rights.

The ideology of human rights

One consequence of the categorisation of human rights into civil and political rights in contrast to economic, social and cultural rights has been the delineation of these rights as either "individual" or "collective" rights. This dichotomy has had major implications for the approach to human rights during most of the post-war period.

The polarisation of views on the nature of human rights between the West and the former Communist bloc was largely premised on the Marxist argument which characterised civil and political rights as essentially bourgeois constructs which erroneously granted too great a prominence to the individual's place in society. Collective rights, on the other hand, were readily endorsed as validating the primacy of state dominance of economic and social life, often at the expense of the individual.

Not surprisingly, traditional legal arguments as to the primacy of the state over the individual as a subject of international law and the doctrine of non-interference, in particular Article 2(7) of the UN Charter, were often used to bolster support for this restrictive view of the acceptable parameters of human rights practice.

The practical implications of this position was that it led to the undermining of the observance of the basic political and civil rights of the individual. It also led to the acceptance of the view that the State, in carrying out its primary responsibility for ensuring the enjoyment of collective rights, could impose restrictions on the enjoyment of civil and political rights, for which it could not be held accountable at the international level. Any attempts to impose accountability were categorically rejected as being a pretext for imperialist interventions in the affairs of states.

The other end of the political spectrum asserted the view that the state had no inherent responsibility to advance economic, social and cultural rights. Rather, the pursuit of collective rights was for each person to pursue in accordance with their individual capacities and talents, the assumption being that these rights were not true "human rights" in the same way that civil and political rights were.

These collective rights were simply regarded as aspirations whose realisation would vary as between states on the basis of prevailing economic and social conditions, and there was.certainly no obligation on states to guarantee the economic, social and cultural welfare of their citizens. The basic role of government was therefore to ensure the protection of individual rights in order to secure for the individual a free, orderly and secure society in which to pursue their individual interests.

Given these disparate views, it was therefore not surprising that international debates on human rights for most of the post war period were influenced by the ideological tensions of the Cold War. Similar tensions are now evident in connection with the North-South approaches to the debate.

The "Asian Values" debate

In recent years a number of regional leaders have been critical of what they perceive as "Western" concepts of human rights and attempts to interfere in their countries' internal affairs. Proponents of "Asian values" argue either that, in developing economies, economic and social rights are more important than political and civil rights; or that a "Western preoccupation" with (individual) civil and political rights threatens to undermine the social cohesion of a more communitarian tradition.

However, given the diversity of political ideologies, cultures and histories in the region, it is perhaps not surprising that there is currently no consensus on a comprehensive definition of "Asian values". The Republic of Korea's President, Kim Dae-Jung, himself a veteran human rights campaigner, emphasised during a speech to the International League for Human Rights in New York in June 1998 that

> *"Actions infringing upon the dignity of human beings should not be tolerated. Regional or cultural characteristics should no longer serve as excuses for the violation of human rights. We must uphold what history has already proven, that human rights is a universal value."*

Arguments about the cultural relativity of human rights are not restricted to the Asian region. UN Secretary-General, Kofi Annan, addressed the issue when speaking to the Organisation of African Unity in Harare on 2 June 1997:

> *"Some Africans still view the concern of human rights as a rich man's luxury for which Africa is not ready; or even as a conspiracy, imposed by the industrialized West. I find these thoughts demeaning - demeaning of the yearning for human dignity that resides in every African heart."*

The Bangkok Declaration on Human Rights, which was adopted by the governments of forty Asian countries at the conclusion of the UN regional meeting for Asia of the World Conference on Human Rights on 2 April 1993, reaffirmed governments' commitment to the principles contained in the UN Charter and the UDHR and encouraged the ratification of international human rights instruments, in particular the ICCPR and the ICESCR. The Declaration recognised human rights as "universal in nature" while acknowledging that they nonetheless had to be considered "in the context of national and regional particularities and various historical, cultural and religious backgrounds". It also reaffirmed the interdependence and indivisibility of political, civil, economic, social and cultural rights, as well as the right to development as a "universal and inalienable right and an integral part of fundamental.human rights". The Declaration affirmed that economic and social progress facilitated the growth of democracy and the promotion and protection of human rights. It also upheld the principles of national sovereignty and "non-interference in the internal affairs of states" and urged the promotion of human rights by cooperation and consensus, not confrontation and conditionality.

A meeting of more than one hundred Asian human rights NGOs in Bangkok shortly before the UN regional meeting for Asia took a somewhat different view. NGOs took a stronger line on the issue of "universality" than did governments, asserting that human rights are universal, and equally rooted in different cultures. Nor did the NGOs regard the advocacy of human rights as encroaching on national sovereignty. While they supported cultural pluralism, the NGOs condemned "those cultural practices which derogate from universally accepted human rights, including women's rights." Like the Bangkok NGO Declaration, the Asian Human Rights Commission's (a Hong Kong based NGO) 1997 draft of an Asian Charter on Human Rights rejects cultural relativism

-Cultural traditions affect the way in which a society organises relationships within itself, but they do not detract from the universalism of rights which are primarily concerned with the relationship of citizens with the state and the inherent dignity of persons and groups.

The Universal Declaration of Human Rights - a review?

At various times, especially in the lead up to the 50th

Anniversary, there have been calls for a review of the Universal Declaration of Human Rights, on the basis that it is outdated or that it was formulated by "superpowers" who did not understand the needs of poor countries. Few countries, however, have explicitly supported this call. Australia's Foreign Minister, Mr Downer, reaffirmed Australia's support for the UDHR as it stands at the Association of South East Asian Nations (ASEAN) Post Ministerial Conference in Kuala Lumpur in late July 1997.

The Declaration contains no provisions in relation to its review or amendment. As it was adopted by the UN General Assembly, only the General Assembly could agree to such a review, and at this stage it seems unlikely that the necessary international support could be achieved for such an action. The UN High Commissioner for Human Rights, Mary Robinson, remarked in her keynote address to an Asia-Pacific Human Rights Symposium held in Tokyo in January 1998 that the Universal Declaration:

> *"can be seen to embody the legal, moral and philosophical beliefs held true by all peoples and because it applies to all... Its universal vocation to protect the dignity of every human being has captured the imagination of humanity. It is this vision which explains the enduring mission of the Declaration and its unsurpassable dominance as a statement of legal principles. We tamper with it at our peril."*

There has been no formal proposal for such a review in the context of the 50th Anniversary..

Human rights and national sovereignty

A fundamental concern of all states, and indeed one of the basic tenets of traditional international law, has been the notion of the national sovereignty of states and the related proscription against states interfering in the domestic affairs of other states. Given the primacy and universality which the UN and the international community have now accorded to the universal enjoyment of human rights, there is clearly a need to reconcile the notions of national sovereignty and the related principle of non-interference with the view that the observance of human rights is a matter of international concern.

Article 2(7) of the UN Charter recognises that there is a duty of non-intervention in the "essentially" domestic affairs of states. In the field of human rights, however, it has increasingly become recognised through state practice since 1948 that this concept has its limits insofar as international scrutiny of human rights violations is concerned. This is because the international community has now accepted that human rights are a legitimate international issue, warranting the scrutiny and criticism by states of human rights abuses in other countries. Articles 55 and 56 of the Charter can be read as expressly conceding that human rights are a legitimate issue for consideration at the international level, a principle reaffirmed in the 1993 Vienna Declaration.

It is therefore increasingly rare to find countries rejecting out of hand human rights representations by other countries, or other forms of international scrutiny, on the basis that these actions constitute an unacceptable interference in their internal affairs. Certainly, any country which has accepted a human rights treaty, whether or not embodying a complaints procedure, cannot use this argument since it has expressly agreed to be bound by the terms of the treaty. In addition, there is also a view that many human rights instruments have become, over time, accepted as part of customary international law, such as the UDHR. This means that a country cannot claim that the provisions of those instruments do not apply to it.

Despite the acceptance of the overriding importance of human rights, limits still exist, albeit recently becoming less clear, in respect of the extent to which states can interfere in the internal affairs of other states. In particular, it is accepted that direct, unilateral intervention involving force would be regarded as illegal under international law. Article 2(7) provides an express exception for such action: the power of the UN Security Council to authorise, in accordance with the terms of the Charter, enforcement action in situations which pose a threat to international peace and security.

4

United Nations System and Human Rights

The UN Charter was signed on 26 June 1945 at the San Francisco Conference on International Organisations and came into force on 24 October 1945. The precursor to the Charter and the UN system was the 1942 Declaration of the United Nations, which was originally signed by 26 states in Washington DC in 1942 and by another 21 by the end of the Second World War. The 1942 Declaration was followed by the 1944 Dumbarton Oaks proposals for the creation of a new world body. Following San Francisco, this body came to be known as the United Nations. Australia was an original member, having been admitted to the UN on 1 November 1945.

The fundamental objective of the UN Charter is the goal of ensuring international peace and security - "saving succeeding generations from the scourge of war" as stated in the Preamble. Nevertheless, the universal promotion and protection of human rights was also recognised as a central tenet of the new UN system. Indeed, the two are closely related. There are therefore several key provisions in the UN Charter referring to human rights, which form the basis of the modern law and practice of human rights. The most important of these provisions are -Article 1, which defines one of the UN's objectives to be "....promoting and encouraging respect for human rights and for fundamental freedoms for all without distinction as to race, sex, language or religion"

Article 13, stating that the responsibilities, functions and powers of the General Assembly shall include "assisting in the realization of human rights and fundamental freedoms for all....".

Article 55, which describes the purposes of the UN in international cooperation including "universal respect for, and observance of human rights and fundamental freedoms for all without discrimination as to race, sex, language, or religion"

Article 56, which contains a pledge by all UN members "to take joint and separate action in cooperation with the Organization for the achievement of the purposes set forth in Article 55"

Article 62, which contains similar provisions describing the responsibilities, functions and powers of the Economic and Social Council (ECOSOC) and Article 76 which describes the International Trusteeship System Article 68, which authorises ECOSOC to set up commissions "in economic and social fields and for the promotion of human rights"

While the terms of these provisions may at first appear quite general, they have in fact formed the basis for the extensive and well established UN practice in the field of human rights. This practice in turn has served to establish the parameters of much of contemporary human rights activities. These Charter provisions also have to be interpreted in the light of subsequent state practice; that is, their real meaning and scope can be fully ascertained by looking at the practice which has taken place since 1946 in the main UN forums dealing with human rights. The major UN organs in the human rights field - the General Assembly, the Security Council, ECOSOC, CHR and CSW - are discussed below.

The General Assembly The United Nations General Assembly (UNGA) is the main representative body of the United Nations. It consists of all member states, each of which has one vote. The regular session of UNGA begins each year on the third Tuesday of September and usually continues until mid-December.

Article 13 of the UN Charter declares that one of the functions of the General Assembly is to initiate studies and make recommendations for the purpose of "promoting international cooperation in the economic, social, cultural, educational, and health fields, and assisting in the realization of human rights and fundamental freedoms for all without distinction as to race, sex, language, or religion". For the most part, human rights items on the agenda of the General Assembly originate in sections of the report of ECOSOC which relate to human rights, or in decisions taken by the Assembly at earlier sessions to consider particular matters. Items relating to human rights have also been proposed for inclusion in the Assembly's agenda by the other principal organs of the United Nations, by Member States, as well as by the Secretary-General.

Since the adoption of the Universal Declaration on Human Rights, the Assembly has adopted numerous declarations or conventions concentrating on human rights. Most items relating to human rights are referred by the General Assembly to its Third Committee, which deals with social, humanitarian and cultural matters. Some, however, are considered by the Assembly without reference to a Main Committee. The other Committees of the UNGA are -the First Committee which considers items which have a bearing on political, international security and disarmament issues; the Second Committee which deals with economic and financial matters; the Fourth Committee which deals with special political and decolonisation matters; the Fifth Committee which handles administrative and budgetary questions, including those arising from the consideration of human rights items; and the Sixth Committee which considers legal issues.

Subsidiary bodies of the General Assembly concerned with human rights or whose work may have a human rights dimension include the -- Special Committee on the Situation with regard to the Implementation of the Declaration on the Granting of Independence to Colonial Countries and Peoples, (known as the Special Committee on Decolonisation);

- Special Committee to Investigate Israeli Practices Affecting the Human Rights of the Population of the Occupied Territories;
- Committee on the Exercise of the Inalienable Rights of the Palestinian People; and

The Security Council

By virtue of Article 24 of the UN Charter, the United Nations Security Council has primary responsibility for the maintenance of international peace and security, a function which encompasses the peaceful settlement of disputes and responses to acts threatening international peace and security. The Security Council has wide-ranging enforcement powers, including the power to authorise sanctions, embargoes and all other necessary means (including the use of force) for the purpose of maintaining or restoring international peace and security.

While the Security Council does not have any express powers (or, arguably, jurisdiction) under the UN Charter in relation to the protection of human rights, its mandate with respect to "international peace and security" is sufficiently wide to ensure that its role in human rights and humanitarian affairs in general is potentially quite substantial. For example, the Security Council acted against both Rhodesia and South Africa as a result of their racist policies, and considered the situations in Kashmir (1948), Indonesia (1949) and the Congo (1964) after human rights concerns were raised by member states..As recent history in Iraq, Somalia the former Yugoslavia and Rwanda has demonstrated, the systematic violation of human rights is often directly or indirectly related to threats to international peace and security. In such circumstances, the Council has taken mandatory measures which have had direct implications for the protection of human rights in various parts of the world. Resolution 688 of April 1991 was the basis for the establishment of "safe havens" for the Kurdish minority in Iraq and is an important illustration of the role the Security Council is capable of playing in the human rights field. The same observation can be made with respect to the creation, pursuant to Security Council resolutions, of the International Criminal Tribunals for the former Yugoslavia and Rwanda which have jurisdiction over serious violations of international humanitarian law.

The Economic and Social Council

The United Nations is charged by its Charter with promoting in the economic and social fields, among other concerns, a universal respect for and observance of human rights and fundamental freedoms for all without distinction as to race, sex, language or religion.

Under Article 62 of the United Nations Charter, the Economic and Social Council (ECOSOC) may make recommendations for the purpose of promoting respect for, and observance of, human rights and fundamental freedoms for all. It may also prepare draft conventions for submission to the General Assembly and call international conferences on human rights matters.

Pursuant to Article 68, ECOSOC "shall set up commissions in economic and social fields and for the protection of human rights". To assist it in dealing with items relating to human rights, the Council established, in accordance with this mandate, two functional committees: the Commission on Human Rights (CHR) and the Commission on the Status of Women (CSW).

ECOSOC, which is composed of 54 members, holds one substantive session annually, limited to four weeks in July, in alternate years in New York and Geneva. Elections, appointments and nominations take place at a resumed organisational session normally in late April/early May. Human rights items are referred to ECOSOC for discussion through the Commission of Human Rights.

ECOSOC has also established ad hoc committees composed of representatives of member states, experts nominated by their governments, or outstanding personalities serving in their personal capacity. The Council has also, on occasion, appointed or authorised the Secretary-General to appoint special rapporteurs or committees of experts to prepare reports on technical subjects.

One of ECOSOC's functions at its substantive session is to receive and consider the annual report of CHR. This report, usually adopted by consensus, is divided into two parts: a main section which includes all the recommendations and resolutions of the CHR as well as voting records and statements made, and a second part including a more limited number of specific items such as draft decisions arising from CHR's work (such as decisions involving financial implications of CHR resolutions), or those which require a higher level of decision-making than CHR (such as the.appointment of special rapporteurs, the mandates of various bodies and the passage of draft instruments to UNGA).

In the context of the discussion on reform of the UN system, ECOSOC has commenced a process of review of the mandates, composition, functions and working methods of its functional commissions and expert groups and bodies, with a view to making ECOSOC itself more action-oriented.

Commission on Human Rights

The Commission on Human Rights was established by ECOSOC in 1946, and has since met annually. It is the main body dealing with human rights issues and has a wide mandate to deal with any matter relating to human rights.

The Commission makes studies, prepares recommendations and drafts international instruments relating to human rights. It also undertakes special tasks assigned to it by the General Assembly or ECOSOC, including the investigation of allegations concerning violations of human rights and the handling of communications relating to such violations. It cooperates closely with all other United Nations bodies having competence in the field of human rights. In addition, it assists ECOSOC in the coordination of activities concerning human rights in the United Nations system. The Commission has also, over the years, transformed itself from a standard-setting body into one which can respond to human rights violations and pursue a wide range of other measures to promote and protect human rights.

The Commission, originally made up of 18 members whose first task had been drafting the International Bill of Human Rights, is now composed of the representatives of 53

Member States elected for three-year terms. It meets each year in Geneva for a period of six weeks and operates under the Rules of Procedure of Functional Commissions of ECOSOC. Only members of the Commission, or their alternates, have the right to vote. The Commission may, however, invite any state to participate in its deliberations on any matter of particular concern to that state.

Specialised agencies and certain other intergovernmental organisations may participate in the Commission's deliberations on questions of concern to them, and non-governmental organisations in consultative status with ECOSOC may designate authorised representatives to sit as observers at public meetings of the Commission. In practice, the Commission has been quite liberal in granting bodies the right to address it.

Since 1992, the Commission has the authority to meet in special sessions whenever a majority of its members so decide. It was given the ability as part of an arrangement by which CHR's membership was also increased from 43 to 53. Since then, it has met in special session on a number of occasions, including to consider the situation in the former Yugoslavia and Rwanda.

To assist in its work, the Commission has established a number of subsidiary bodies, including the Sub-Commission on Prevention of Discrimination and Protection of Minorities. The Sub-Commission assists, and reports to, CHR in various areas, as its mandate is not limited to minorities or discrimination issues. (The Sub-.Commission has, for example, appointed special rapporteurs on terrorism, states of emergency, privatisation of prisons and income distribution.)

In recent years, CHR has also set up organs to investigate human rights problems in specific countries and territories as well as on thematic situations. At present, the following Working Groups exist:

- the Working Group on the Human Rights of Migrants;
- the Working Group on Structural Adjustment Programmes and Economic, Social and Cultural Rights;
- the Working Group on Situations;
- the Working Group on Arbitrary Detention;
- the Working Group on Enforced or Involuntary Disappearances; and
- the Working Group on the Right to Development.

The Commission has also established informal open-ended working groups to assist in the drafting of international declarations and conventions, for example:

- the Working Group on the Optional Protocol to the Convention Against Torture and Other Cruel, Inhuman or Degrading Treatment or Punishment;
- the Working Group on the Draft Declaration on the Rights of Indigenous Peoples;
- the Working Group on a Draft Optional Protocol to the CROC on Involvement of Children in Armed Conflicts; and
- the Working Group on a Draft Optional Protocol to the CROC on the Sale of Children, Child Prostitution and Child Pornography.

In discussing the work of CHR and ECOSOC, reference needs to be made to the various mechanisms which have been established to assist these bodies in the promotion and protection of human rights, including by employing a variety of methods for dealing with violations of human rights. These mechanisms include fact-finding by experts (consisting of special rapporteurs, representatives or other designees appointed by the Commission) to study the situation of human rights either in specific countries or on a thematic basis.

The acceptance of these mechanisms by the UN community heralded important steps in the international acceptance of "domestic" human rights issues as legitimate matters for international scrutiny. Previously, UN involvement in the human rights affairs of member states was strenuously opposed by states on the grounds that this would constitute interference in a state's domestic affairs and thus be in breach of Article 2(7) of the UN Charter. Given such opposition, cases where scrutiny of a.state's human rights record were successful were usually predicated on the UN first finding that these human rights violations constituted threats to international peace and security. For example, this was the way apartheid in South Africa was placed on the UN's agenda. On the other hand, supporters of these procedures argued that these mechanisms had established a proper balance between the often conflicting implications of Article 2(7) and the UN's human rights mandate.

By passing resolutions establishing these mechanisms, CHR and ECOSOC made a qualitative jump in respect of UN involvement in human rights, insofar as they were asserting that what had hitherto been regarded as essentially domestic matters could now be scrutinised by other countries in the forums of the UN. Furthermore, there did not have to be a finding of a threat to international peace and security to activate such mechanisms, since the seriousness and scale of the human rights violations - "a consistent pattern of gross and systematic violations of human rights" - were regarded of themselves as being sufficient to justify international interest and condemnation. The most important of these mechanisms are -The 1503 Communications Procedure The 1235 Procedure.

The 1503 Communications procedure

This process, used to examine reports of human rights

violations, is called a "1503 Procedure" because it was established pursuant to the 1970 ECOSOC Resolution 1503. It seeks to deal with the examination of country situations rather than resolving individuals' complaints. The procedure applies to all states.

From the time of the first session of the Commission on Human Rights in 1947, there was clearly a need for some form of communications procedure. In 1959, ECOSOC Resolution 728F established that confidential communications relating to human rights violations should be sent to both CHR and the Sub-Commission on Prevention of Discrimination and Protection of Minorities. States which were the subject of such communications could receive and respond to these communications. In 1967, ECOSOC, in its Resolution 1235, authorised CHR and the Sub-Commission to examine information relevant to gross violations of human rights and fundamental freedoms in all countries. CHR was given the additional right to make thorough studies of situations revealing a consistent pattern of violations of human rights, and report and make recommendations to ECOSOC: the so called "1235 Procedure".

The 1503 Procedure was established to deal with "communications relating to violation of human rights and fundamental freedoms, indicating a consistent pattern of serious violations". Any person, group or NGO may invoke the procedure if they have reliable knowledge of such violations. Once they have submitted their communications, the originators do not become involved at any stage in the implementation of the process; in fact, they may not even be informed of the outcome unless it is made public. The process for handling 1503 communications is as follows:.· The authors lodge their communications with the UN Secretariat, copies are sent to the states concerned and summaries handed to members of the Sub-Commission, which meets as a five-member Working

Group in closed session before the annual session of the Sub-Commission.

The Working Group considers both the communications and states' replies, if provided, and decides by a majority vote which situations warrant referral to the Sub-Commission. Criteria used in this "sifting process" are:

— the communications indicate a consistent pattern of gross violations of human rights and fundamental freedoms

— individual cases are only relevant if they relate to such a pattern or situation

— the information is reliable and direct, or second-hand if properly corroborated by evidence

— the evidence is not anonymous.

Communications approved by the Working Group are then considered by the Sub-Commission in closed session, which decides - again using the "consistent pattern of gross violations" criterion - whether these should be submitted to CHR.

In order to decide which communications may be accepted for examination, the Sub-Commission has drawn up rules of procedure. These specify that:

· The aim of the communication must not be inconsistent with the principles of the United Nations Charter, the Universal Declaration of Human Rights or other applicable human rights treaties, and must not show political motivations.

· Communications will be admitted only if their consideration shows there are reasonable grounds to believe (also taking into account any replies sent by the governments concerned) that there is a consistent pattern of gross and reliably attested violations of human rights and fundamental freedoms.

- Communications may be admitted when they come from people, whether individuals or groups, who claim to be victims of human rights violations. They may also be admitted when they come from any person or group of people which has direct, reliable knowledge of violations. When an NGO presents communications on violations, it does so on the condition that it is acting in good faith in accordance with recognised principles of human rights, and that it has direct, reliable evidence of the situation it is describing.
- Anonymous communications are inadmissible, as are those based only on reports in the mass media..
- Each communication must describe the facts, the purpose of the petition, and the rights that have been violated.
- Domestic remedies must have been exhausted before a communication is considered, unless it can be convincingly shown that these would be ineffective or would extend over an unreasonable length of time. These rules of procedure seek to avoid overlapping with other existing procedures, and the repeated submission of communications already dealt with by the United Nations.

Before it resumes the session each year, CHR appoints a 5-person group to meet in closed session to study the situation in question and draw up draft decisions on each situation for adoption by consensus in CHR. All CHR members are provided with the communications and the draft decision. They then discuss the country situation behind closed doors, although countries which are the subject of discussion are also invited to attend if they are not CHR members. CHR can decide to keep the situation under review (including, subject to the states' consent, by appointing an expert to examine the situation), or it may decide to remove the item from the agenda. While these meetings are confidential, the names of countries subject to or removed from the agenda are made public. These CHR decisions may be referred to ECOSOC, which may make public recommendations to the states which are the subject of such decisions.

Special Rapporteurs

Another well established process in place for examining human rights violations is the 1235 Procedure, established in 1967. Under this mechanism, the Commission can place country situations on its public agenda (Item 10). In addition, CHR has, subject to ECOSOC's approval, the power to appoint "special rapporteurs". Special rapporteurs have now become an established part of human rights monitoring, playing an important and respected role in the UN human rights field. There are essentially two types of rapporteurs established under this procedure - "country rapporteurs" and "thematic rapporteurs".

The mandates of special rapporteurs vary: most invariably involve a supervisory role, while others have the task of elaborating concepts or specific rights. All rapporteurs present annual reports to CHR which set out their findings. Some rapporteurs, such as the Special Rapporteur on Torture, also have an investigatory role, with authority to examine state practices in the relevant field (including by receiving and investigating specific allegations of abuses and making urgent calls to governments on these cases).

The special rapporteur mechanism needs to be distinguished from that of a "special representative". The latter is expressly appointed by the UN Secretary-General, to whom the representative reports directly and whose work is usually considered at CHR under the Advisory Services Item. Special representatives have been established for Cambodia (Hammarberg), Iran (Copithorne) and Rwanda (Moussalli),

Impact on armed conflict on children (Otunnu) and Internally displaced persons (Deng).

The Commission has also established under these procedures various working groups, which report directly to CHR. The first one was established in 1980 - the "supervisory" Working Group on Enforced and Involuntary Disappearances. This has since been followed by several others, including the Working Groups on Arbitrary Detention, the Right to Development and the Human Rights of Migrants. CHR has also established "standard-setting" working groups mandated to draft international instruments: examples include the Working Group drafting an Optional Protocol for the Convention against Torture and the Working Group on the Draft Declaration on the Rights of Indigenous Peoples.

Office of the High Commissioner for Human Rights

The Office of the High Commissioner for Human Rights, which forms part of the UN Office in Geneva, is the focal point for the human rights activities of the United Nations and is the primary organisational unit within the UN Secretariat for the implementation of the UN's human rights program. The Centre for Human Rights.was subsumed into the Office of the High Commissioner in September 1997, following the appointment of Mrs Mary Robinson to the position of High Commissioner for Human Rights. The human rights program of the Office of the High Commissioner is based on the following three objectives:

- the preparation of international standards;
- the implementation of those standards through monitoring and assistance; and
- the promotion of those standards through education and information.

Within this framework, emphasis is given to the elimination of discrimination and to the promotion of the enjoyment of all human rights. The program also emphasises issues relating to human rights and development and to the problems and protection of especially vulnerable groups such as children, indigenous populations, migrant workers, minorities and the extremely poor.

The functions of the Office of the High Commissioner for Human Rights are as follows:

- to promote the universal enjoyment of all human rights;
- to play a leading role in human rights issues and emphasise the importance of human rights at the international and national levels;
- to promote international cooperation on human rights;
- to stimulate and coordinate action for human rights throughout the United Nations system;
- to promote universal ratification and implementation of international standards;
- to assist in the development of new norms;
- to support human rights organs and treaty monitoring bodies;
- to respond to serious violations of human rights;
- to undertake preventive action to protect human rights;
- to promote the establishment of national human rights infrastructures;
- to undertake human rights field activities and operations; and
- to provide education, information, advisory services and technical assistance in the field of human rights.

A significant current component of the work of the Office is the maintenance of field operations in Burundi, Rwanda and the former Yugoslavia, which have experienced particularly grave and widespread breaches of human rights in recent times. Field.offices are also maintained in a number of human rights "flashpoints" including Cambodia, Colombia, the Democratic Republic of the Congo and Gaza.

As Head of the Office, the High Commissioner for Human Rights coordinates the human rights program with related activities within the Secretariat and the United Nations system, and represents the Secretary-General at meetings of human rights organs and at other human rights events. The High Commissioner for Human Rights also promotes the ratification and application of international human rights conventions, and assists in the exercise of the humanitarian good offices of the Secretary-General.

Commission on the Status of Women

The Commission on the Status of Women (CSW) was established by the Economic and Social Council in 1946. Its functions are:

- to prepare recommendations and reports to ECOSOC on promoting women's rights in the political, economic, civil, social and educational fields; and
- to make recommendations to ECOSOC on urgent problems requiring immediate attention in the field of women's rights, with the object of implementing the principle that men and women shall have equal rights, and to develop proposals to give effect to such recommendations.

The Commission, which meets annually for a session of two weeks in New York, comprises 45 members, elected for four-year terms. Australia is currently an observer at the

Commission having served as a member during 1955-57; 1961-63; 1967-69; 1983-1990; and 1993-96. The Commission adopts its own resolutions and decisions and prepares draft resolutions and decisions for consideration by ECOSOC.

The Commission has two working groups:

- The Working Group on Communications on the Status of Women (established by ECOSOC resolution 1983/27) which meets in closed session during each session of the Commission to consider communications received, including the replies of governments, on discriminative practices against women; and
- an open-ended Working Group of the UN Commission to draft an optional protocol to the Convention on the Elimination of All Forms of Discrimination Against Women (CEDAW). The principal purpose of the Protocol would be to establish an individual complaints mechanism, similar to those already in existence pursuant to the International Covenant on Civil and Political Rights, the Convention on the Elimination of all Forms of Racial Discrimination, and the Convention Against Torture and Other Cruel or Inhuman Degrading Treatment or Punishment. The fourth meeting of the Working Group is to be held in March 1999..While not having a specific human rights mandate, the international organisations discussed below often have a major role to play in the international practice of human rights.

United Nations Educational Scientific and Cultural Organization

The purpose of the United Nations Educational Scientific and Cultural Organization (UNESCO), as laid down in Article 1 of its Constitution, is -fundamental freedoms which are affirmed for the peoples of the world, without to contribute to peace and security by promoting collaboration among the nations through education, science and culture in order to further universal respect for justice, for the rule of law and for the human rights and distinction of race, sex, language or religion, by the Charter of the United Nations.

In addition to carrying out a programme involving many forms of direct action designed to deal with the complex problems encountered in the development of education, science and culture, UNESCO has prepared several conventions and recommendations relating to human rights. For example, the 1960 Convention against Discrimination in Education was adopted by the General Conference of UNESCO in 1960. More recently, on 11 November 1997, the General Conference of UNESCO adopted a Universal Declaration on the Human Genome and Human Rights. This Declaration is ground-breaking in international human rights policy as it seeks to balance the rights of persons subjected to human genetic research (upholding the principle of respect for human dignity) and the freedom to conduct research - an attribute of the freedom of thought.

In particular, UNESCO has also established a Commission on Conventions and Recommendations mandated to receive and hear complaints from groups or individuals about human rights violations in member states in the educational, scientific, cultural, and information fields. These matters, in accordance with UNESCO terminology, are either "cases" (that is, specific cases) or "questions" involving more serious human rights situations. The latter set of matters is required to be heard in public sessions by the Executive Board and the General Conference.

United Nations High Commissioner for Refugees

The Office of the United Nations High Commissioner for

Refugees (UNHCR) was established by the UN General Assembly and commenced operations on 1 January 1951. It is entrusted with providing international protection, under United Nations auspices, to refugees falling within its competence, and of seeking permanent solutions for the problem of refugees by assisting governments to facilitate the voluntary repatriation of such refugees, or their assimilation within new national communities. It seeks to fulfil this mandate by -- promoting the conclusion and ratification of international conventions for the protection of refugees, as well as supervising their application and proposing amendments to them;.

- promoting, through special agreements with governments, the execution of measures to improve the situation of refugees and to reduce the number requiring protection;
- assisting governmental and private efforts to promote voluntary repatriation or assimilation within new national communities;
- promoting the admission of refugees to the territories of states;
- endeavouring to obtain permission for refugees to transfer their assets, especially those necessary for their resettlement;
- obtaining information from governments concerning the number and conditions of refugees in their territories and the laws and regulations concerning them;
- keeping in close touch with the governments and intergovernmental organisations concerned;
- establishing contact with private organisations dealing with refugee questions; and
- facilitating the co-ordination of efforts of private organisations concerned with the welfare of refugees.

In addition, UNHCR may engage in repatriation and resettlement activities at the request of the General Assembly. It also performs certain functions to assist stateless persons under the Convention on the Reduction of Statelessness.

International Labour Organisation

Since its establishment under the 1919 Treaty of Versailles as an autonomous institution associated with the League of Nations, the International Labour Organisation's (ILO) main concern has been the formulation of international labour standards and their effective implementation. Yet the human rights dimensions of the work of the ILO are evident from the ILO Constitution, which recognises that labour is not a commodity and that all human beings - irrespective of race, creed or sex -have the right to pursue both their material well-being and their spiritual development in conditions of freedom, dignity, economic security and equal opportunity.

The ILO consists of an International Labour Conference, a Governing Body (the ILO's executive council), an International Labour Office (which acts as the secretariat), regional conferences, committees and groups of experts. The International Labour Conference meets annually in Geneva to debate global social and labour problems. Each member state is entitled to be represented by four.delegates, two of whom should be representative of the government, while the other two should be representative of employers' and workers' groups.

The ILO has gradually built up a significant body of over 360 international labour conventions and recommendations. (The ILO conventions are legally binding, whilst the recommendations act as important guidelines for states.) Several instruments deal with human rights issues such as protection of freedom of association and the right to organise;

prohibition of forced and child labour and promotion of non-discrimination in employment and occupation.

National implementation of ILO instruments is supervised by a 20 member Committee of Experts on the Application of Conventions and Recommendations and the tripartite Conference Committee on the Application of Standards, both of which were established pursuant to a 1926 ILO Conference resolution. In addition, Article 24 of the ILO Constitution allows for representations to be initiated by workers' or employers' associations in cases of alleged non-observance by states of their ILO obligations. Inter-state complaints can also be initiated pursuant to Article 26 of the Constitution. Finally, a special procedure in relation to complaints concerning infringements of the right to freedom of association - the 9 member Committee on Freedom of Association - has existed since its establishment in 1950 by an ILO Governing Body/ ECOSOC decision.

International Law Commission

The International Law Commission (ILC) was established in 1947 by the UN General Assembly pursuant to Resolution 174(II), with an original membership of 15 persons. Composed of international legal experts, it has the function of encouraging the progressive development of international law and its codification in accordance with Article 13 of UN Charter. The ILC presently consists of 34 persons, elected for a 5 year period from nominations by UN Members.

While the main focus of the ILC is in the international legal field, in particular the drafting of conventions in areas where law is not sufficiently developed, it is inevitable that the work of the Commission should often have an impact in relation to the development or strengthening of human rights standards. Areas where the ILC plays a key role in the development of human rights law include statelessness, state responsibility, nationality and international criminal law. The ILC developed the draft Statute for the International Criminal Court. An Australian, Professor James Crawford, is currently serving on the Commission.

Food and Agriculture Organization

A basic purpose of the Food and Agriculture Organization is ". . . contributing towards an expanding world economy and ensuring humanity's freedom from hunger". As such, the agency is mainly concerned with raising levels of nutrition and standards of living, securing improvements in the efficiency of the production and distribution of food and agricultural products, bettering the condition of rural populations, thereby contributing towards an expanding world economy..

FAO's activities are designed to help solve one of the fundamental problems of mankind - the overall provision of the world's food supply. The Freedom from Hunger Campaign, launched by FAO in 1960, spread public knowledge of development problems in the agency's fields of concern and mobilised public opinion for increased development efforts.

World Health Organization

The preamble to the Constitution of the World Health Organization declares that the enjoyment of the highest attainable standard of health is a fundamental right of every human being and that governments have a responsibility for the health of their peoples, which can only be fulfilled by the provision of adequate health and social measures.

The WHO serves as the coordinating authority on international health work. It maintains certain necessary international health services, promotes and conducts research in the field of health, and works to improve standards of teaching in the health, medical and related professions.

Bodies established pursuant to United Nations Human Rights Instruments The bodies described above are all standing bodies of the UN established in accordance with and pursuant to the provisions of the UN Charter; they are thus often characterised as "Charter-based" bodies. These are distinguished from so-called "treaty-based" bodies, which have been specifically established pursuant to the provisions of the major UN human rights instruments. Their role is essentially to monitor and supervise states parties' compliance with their obligations under the relevant treaties.

There are six major UN treaty-based bodies, as follows (the treaties to which they relate are in parentheses):

- The Committee on the Elimination of Racial Discrimination (CERD)
- The Human Rights Committee (ICCPR)
- The Committee on Economic, Social and Cultural Rights (ICESCR)
- The Committee on the Elimination of Discrimination against Women (CEDAW)
- The Committee against Torture (CAT); and
- The Committee on the Rights of the Child (CROC)

In addition, the 1990 Convention on the Protection of the Rights of all Migrant Workers and Members of their Family, provides, pursuant to Article 72, for the establishment of an eighth treaty-based Committee to review the application of this Convention. With only 9 states parties as at October 1998, this

Convention has not yet entered into force..Committee on the Elimination of Racial Discrimination This Committee, established in 1970 in accordance with Article 8 of the Convention of the Elimination of All Forms of Racial Discrimination, consists of 18 experts of 'high moral standing and acknowledged impartiality', elected by states parties from among their nationals. Members are elected for a four-year term by secret ballot at a meeting of the states parties, and serve in their personal capacity. The tasks of the Committee, as set out in part II of the Convention, are:

- to consider reports on the legislative, judicial, administrative or other measures states parties have adopted to give effect to the provisions of the Convention;
- to make suggestions and general recommendations based on the examination of those reports and other information;
- to assist in settling disputes among states parties concerning the application of the Convention; and
- to receive and consider communications from individuals or groups of individuals within the jurisdiction of those states parties which have recognised the competence of the Committee under Article 14.

When necessary, the Committee may establish an ad hoc conciliation commission to make available its good offices to states parties in a dispute concerning the application of the Convention, with a view to an amicable settlement on the basis of respect for the Convention. Such a commission would report to the Committee on all questions of fact relevant to the issue between the parties, and make recommendations for the amicable settlement of the dispute.

In accordance with Article 15 of the Convention, the Committee also considers copies of petitions, copies of reports, and other information on racial discrimination relating to Trust and Non-Self-Governing Territories and to all other Territories to which General Assembly resolution 1514(XV) applies, transmitted to it by the Trusteeship Council and by the Special Committee on Decolonisation.

The Committee met for the first time on 19 January 1970. Since that time, it has normally held two sessions each year and has reported annually to the General Assembly. At each session, the Committee examines the information placed at its disposal by states parties to the Convention and by the United Nations bodies concerned with dependent Territories. Representatives of states parties are usually present at the meetings of the Committee when their reports, pursuant to Article 9 of the Convention, are examined, and may answer questions or submit additional information. Australia's eighth periodic report was submitted in 1992 and its ninth periodic report was submitted in 1993.

A combined 10th, 11th and 12th report will be submitted early in 1999..The Committee may also comment on situations involving racial discrimination or draw them to the attention of the General Assembly. It indicates matters on which it would like to receive detailed information from states parties. The Committee introduced Early Warning Measures and Urgent Action Procedures in 1994 which has since involved consideration of some 15 countries. There are no rules governing the application of the procedure which is on a case-by-case basis. In addition, the Committee may request information or conduct inquiries into the situation in particular countries on the basis of a specific complaint by another state or an individual.

As at October 1998 there were 151 states parties to the Convention on the Elimination of All Forms of Racial Discrimination, 24 of which have recognised the competence of the Committee under Article 14 to receive and consider communications from individuals or groups of individuals. Australia lodged its Article 14 declaration in February 1993. Human Rights Committee

The Human Rights Committee was established in 1977 in accordance with Article 28 of the International Covenant on Civil and Political Rights. It consists of 18 members of high moral character and recognised competence in the field of human rights elected by states parties from among their nationals. Members are elected for a four-year term by secret ballot at a meeting of the states parties, and serve in their personal capacity. The tasks of the Committee, as set out in Articles 40 to 45 of the Covenant, are: · to study initial and subsequent periodic state reports which set out the measures states parties have adopted to give effect to the rights recognised in the ICCPR and on the progress made in the enjoyment of those rights;

- to transmit its reports and such "general comments" made under Article 40(4) as it may consider appropriate to states parties;
- to perform certain functions with a view to settling disputes among states parties concerning the application of the ICCPR, provided that those parties have recognised the competence of the Committee to that effect; and
- when necessary to establish an ad hoc conciliation commission to make available its good offices to states parties involved in a dispute concerning the application of the ICCPR, with a view to a friendly solution of the matter on the basis of respect for the ICCPR. Such a commission must submit a report to the Committee Chairman, not later than 12 months after having been seized of the matter, for communication to the states parties concerned.

The Committee examines reports from states parties to the ICCPR on the measures taken by them to give effect to the rights recognised in the ICCPR, on the progress made in the enjoyment of those rights and on any factors and difficulties affecting the implementation of the ICCPR. As in the case of the Committee on the CERD, state representatives are allowed to be present at meetings of the HRC when their reports are examined. The Committee may also inform a state party from which it.decides to seek further information that it may authorise its representative to be present at a specified meeting. The representative should be able to answer questions put by the Committee and may make statements on reports already submitted by their state. Representatives may also submit additional information from their state. The Committee normally holds three sessions each year and reports annually, through ECOSOC, to the General Assembly.

In its capacity as a body handling communications, the HRC has two functions -· Receiving state complaints under Article 41 of the ICCPR. A state party must declare that it recognises the competence of the Committee to receive and consider such communications from other states. In these communications, a state party may claim that another state party is not fulfilling its obligations under the ICCPR. Communications received under this article are dealt with in accordance with a special procedure. Although 45 states have submitted to Article 41, no state has ever initiated this procedure.

Receiving individual complaints under the Optional Protocol to the ICCPR. Under this procedure individuals who claim that any of their rights enumerated in the ICCPR have been violated, and who have exhausted all available domestic remedies, may submit written communications to the Human Rights Committee for consideration.

The individual petition - or "communications" - procedure established by the Optional Protocol is subject to the following procedural and threshold requirements: · the communication relates to a state which is a party to both the ICCPR and the Optional Protocol (Article 1); · the communication is in writing and the claimant has exhausted all available domestic remedies (Article 2), unless these remedies have been unreasonably prolonged (Article 5(2));

- the communication is inadmissible if anonymous or held by the Committee to have been an abuse of the rights of submission or incompatible with the provisions of the ICCPR (Article 3);
- No matter can be held admissible until the state which is the subject of the communication has been informed of the communication (Article 4); · The state shall, within six months, present a written statement or explanation clarifying the matter and setting out any remedy adopted (Article 4); and
- The Committee considers the communication in the light of all written material made available by the individual and the state, but shall not consider it where it finds that the same matter is being considered under another international investigation or settlement (Article 5).

When the Committee considers communications received under the Optional Protocol, it has the assistance of a Working Group on Communications, established.at every session and consisting of not more than five of its members. All documents relating to the Committee's work under the Protocol are confidential, and they are examined in closed meetings. The texts of final decisions of the Committee, which are declaratory, are made public. The Committee includes a summary of its activities under the Protocol in its annual report, as required under Article 6.

The Committee has accepted nearly 300 individual complaints and found violations in over 220 of them, involving matters such as disappearances, torture, deprivation of liberty, freedom of movement, and sexual discrimination.

The Committee also regularly establishes a Working Group, made up of not more than five Committee members, to assist it in the drafting of lists of issues in connection with the consideration of states' periodic reports and in the preparation of general comments. These general comments, addressed to the state concerned as required by Article 40(4) of the ICCPR, also summarise the Committee's experience with country reports; promote the goals of implementation of the ICCPR, improved reporting, and inter-state cooperation; and provide comments relating to the application and contents of various articles. General comments are referred to UNGA, ECOSOC and to states parties.

General comments issued by the Committee have, for example, examined questions of sexual equality, public emergencies, the right to life, torture, freedom of expression, detainees, war propaganda, the administration of justice, privacy, and the rights of children and families. These comments are important sources of clarification of the ICCPR since they are often inspired by individual cases referred to the Committee. No states, however, are named in such comments. Through this work, the Committee is developing an important corpus of material relevant to the interpretation and effective implementation of the Covenant.

As at 1 October 1998, there were 140 States Parties to the International Covenant on Civil and Political Rights. Ninety-four states parties have ratified or acceded to the Optional Protocol, and 45 states have made the declaration under article 41 of the Covenant recognising the competence of the Human Rights Committee to consider communications relating to inter-state disputes.

5

Introduction to the World Report on Human Rights

Sovereignty loomed less large in 1999 as an obstacle to stopping and redressing crimes against humanity. Governmental leaders who committed these crimes faced a greater chance of prosecution and even military intervention. The lesson sent is that leaders risk their freedom and control of territory if they commit the most severe human rights abuses.

The year saw significant progress toward an international system of justice available to prosecute these crimes. The Spanish-initiated case against former Chilean dictator General Augusto Pinochet, the first international prosecution of a former head of state since Nuremberg, continued to move through the British courts. The International Criminal Tribunal for the Former Yugoslavia issued the first indictment of a sitting head of state, Yugoslav President Slobodan Milosevic. NATO troops in Bosnia arrested several, though still not the most significant, war-crimes suspects indicted by the tribunal. The International Criminal Tribunal for Rwanda continued its successful prosecution of leading authorities responsible for genocide in that country. The International Criminal Court, the first global institution of justice capable of prosecuting the world's worst human rights offenders, picked up support at an impressive clip; with eighty-nine governments having signed its treaty through October, the question is no longer whether this landmark institution will become operational, but when.

Not only international tribunals but also national courts showed a greater willingness to prosecute severe human rights crimes committed outside their nation's borders. In addition to Britain's and Spain's prosecution of Pinochet, a Swiss military court found a former Rwandan official guilty of war crimes for his role in the 1994 genocide. Already, Germany and Denmark had convicted two Bosnian Serbs and a Bosnian Muslim for atrocities committed during the Bosnian conflict, while Austrian and Swiss courts had tried and acquitted two Bosnian Serbs for such crimes. Similar criminal proceedings are ongoing in at least four other cases in Belgium, France, Germany and the Netherlands. And a senior Iraqi official had to beat a hasty retreat home when public appeals were launched to the governments of Austria and Jordan to arrest him for his role in severe Iraqi repression.

Meanwhile, the international community displayed a new willingness to deploy troops to stop crimes against humanity. In East Timor, intense diplomatic and economic pressure convinced Jakarta to permit belatedly the deployment of a multinational force to halt the scorched-earth campaign of Indonesian army-backed militia. In Kosovo, it took NATO's controversial bombing campaign before Belgrade would acquiesce in the deployment of international troops to stop widespread ethnic slaughter and forced displacement.

These trends mark the beginning of a new era for the human rights movement. Until now, the lack of anything resembling an international criminal justice system restricted the options available to defend human rights. Human rights organizations could shame abusive governments. They could galvanize diplomatic and economic pressure. They could invoke international human rights standards. But rarely could they trigger the prosecution of tyrants or count on governments to use their police powers to enforce human rights law.

Slowly, that appears to be changing. Today, tyrants are increasingly likely to be indicted. As the International Criminal Tribunals for Rwanda and the Former Yugoslavia and various national courts gradually gain custody of indicted suspects, a record of arrest, prosecution and punishment is being built.

Meanwhile, at least in parts of the world, the international community seems more willing to deploy troops to halt massive slaughter. These trends are still halting and replete with problems of consistency and potential misuse. Africa seems to have been particularly neglected. But they foretell an era in which the defense of human rights can move from a paradigm of pressure based on international human rights law to one of law enforcement.

The growing willingness to transcend sovereignty in the face of crimes against humanity hardly means an end to the Westphalian system of government. Sovereign governments retain primary responsibility for preserving order, establishing the rule of law, and protecting human rights.

This duty is important not only in its own right but also to prevent less severe human rights violations from erupting into atrocities-the least costly and most humane strategy. If governments fall short of these responsibilities, the human rights movement can resort to its usual techniques: exposure, denunciation, ostracism, and calls for sanctions.

Yet, the past year suggests that, in the most extreme cases, new tools might be available as well. Human Rights Watch's tenth World Report discusses these substantial changes in the global system for the defense of human right- both the promise they hold and the risks they carry.

Military Intervention

Certainly the most dramatic development in 1999 was the use of military force by regional and international bodies to stop crimes against humanity-that is, the most severe abuses committed as part of a widespread or systematic attack on a civilian population. It was only five years ago that the international community shamefully turned its back on genocide in Rwanda. Twice in the past year, in Kosovo and East Timor, members of the international community deployed troops to halt crimes against humanity. In East Timor, intense diplomatic and economic pressure secured the Indonesian government's consent to the deployment of a multinational force. In Kosovo, NATO bombing produced the Yugoslav government's agreement to the deployment of international troops. The two instances may signal a new readiness on the part of the international community to use extraordinary resources, including troops, to address crimes against humanity that are within its power to stop.

East Timor

After the U.N. announced on September 4 that East Timorese had voted overwhelming for independence in the U.N.-supervised referendum held on August 30, Indonesian army-backed militia went on a rampage of killing, arson, and destruction. Jakarta claimed it was trying to rein in the violence, but the evidence, including many eyewitness accounts, suggested army and police involvement in a coordinated campaign to drive out independent observers and then embark on a scorched-earth campaign that left unknown numbers dead and, in many places, over half of the homes and infrastructure destroyed. Hundreds of thousands of East Timorese were displaced, many of them forcedacross the border into Indonesian West Timor. The challenge to the international community was how to stop this violence and destruction if Jakarta would not.

The international community was rightly faulted for its inadequate precautions to avoid this bloodshed. Eager to take advantage of the window of opportunity afforded by then Indonesian President B.J. Habibie's surprise announcement in January 1999 that his government would allow East Timor to hold a referendum to determine its future, the U.N. in May brokered an agreement that gave the Indonesian government responsibility for maintaining security in East Timor through the referendum period. Instead, in the months leading up to the vote, Indonesian troops repeatedly stood by while local militia, many of which the army itself had organized, engaged in a bloody campaign of intimidation against independence supporters and U.N. workers. The international community, in turn, put inadequate pressure on Jakarta to disarm and demobilize the militia in advance of the referendum.

When massive violence erupted in early September, intervention by international troops was never a realistic option without the Indonesian government's acquiescence. Australia alone was willing to offer troops to lead an intervention, but it refused to act without the U.N. Security Council's approval, and the Security Council was unwilling to endorse military intervention without Jakarta's consent. International efforts thus centered on putting pressure on the Indonesian government either to stop the killing itself or to authorize others to do so.

At first the pressure was applied slowly, because donor governments were concerned that too insistent demands might derail Indonesia's democratization and promote separatism, even though one of the greatest threats to democratization and territorial integrity continued to be the Indonesian military's reluctance to be subjected to the rule of law. The U.N. High Commissioner for Human Rights, Mary Robinson, among others, helped to highlight the atrocities being committed in East Timor. Ultimately, and belatedly, the United States and the European Union, under substantial public pressure, cut off or threatened to terminate access to aid and weapons unless the atrocities stopped. The World Bank and the International Monetary Fund also held up funds because of pressure from donor governments and apparent fear that the violence in East Timor would further discourage international investment in Indonesia's already crippled economy. The message thus was sent that Indonesia could not benefit from international largesse if it was so blatantly flouting international rules prohibiting crimes against humanity. Only Japan among the major donors insisted on placing its economic ties ahead of the imperative of stopping bloodshed, although it did exert diplomatic pressure.

The combined pressure was sufficient to secure Jakarta's consent to the deployment of a multinational force in East Timor, though by then the army's and militia's scorched-earth campaign had left East Timor in ruins and largely depopulated. Moreover, tens of thousands of East Timorese had fled, often under duress, to West Timor, where no international troops were deployed.

In the meantime, the behavior of the unarmed members of the U.N. Mission in East Timor (UNAMET) was exemplary. Their brave sense of duty is best shown by contrasting it with the behavior of the armed U.N. troops defending the Bosnian town of Srebrenica in 1995. The U.N. troops in Srebrenica had abandoned the civilian population of the Security Council-declared "safe area" to be slaughtered by Bosnian Serb troops. Even their Bosnian staff members were forced to leave family members in the hands of the attacking forces. But many UNAMET representatives in East Timor insisted on bringing their Timorese staff with them as they fled toward Dili, the capital, and then refused to be evacuated from their headquarters in Dili until the local staff, their family members, and all Timorese civilians who had taken refuge in the compound were also evacuated.

The "Annan Doctrine"

The extent to which traditional prerogatives of sovereignty have given way in the face of crimes against humanity was well illustrated by the statements of U.N. Secretary-General Kofi Annan. In a widely remarked-upon speech to open the General Assembly on September 20, he insisted that sovereignty must give way to the imperative of stopping crimes against humanity-a courageous stand for a man who leads an organization of governments.

Less noticed, but perhaps more revolutionary, was his statement of September 10 that senior Indonesian officials risked prosecution for crimes against humanity if they did not consent to the deployment of an available multinational force. This was such an important pronouncement that it merits being called the "Annan doctrine."

It has long been established that in certain instances, commanders of military forces can be prosecuted for atrocities committed by their troops. Articulated by the Nuremberg and Tokyo tribunals, this doctrine of "command responsibility" is now codified in the Geneva Conventions and their Protocols. It imposes criminal liability on a commander who knew or had reason to know that troops under his command were committing atrocities and who failed to take "all feasible measures" within his power to stop them.

These "feasible measures" were typically understood to mean ordering or deploying the commander's own security forces to halt abuses. But the emergence of a vigilant human rights movement is among the factors that have perversely encouraged what might be called the "death squad dodge."

To avoid the opprobrium and potential criminal liability that comes with openly committing executions and torture, abusive militaries began to subcontract atrocities to irregular forces which the military could then claim were beyond its control. Examples of this phenomenon can be seen in the "death squads" of Central America in the 1980s, the Colombian and Serbian paramilitaries of the 1990s and, most recently, the militia created in East Timor by the Indonesian army.

Rather than enter into the murky debate about how much control the Indonesian government retained over the militia, Kofi Annan insisted that the government, on pain of criminal liability, either stop the killing itself or consent to the deployment of international troops who were willing to do so.

If Jakarta refused to accept the international community's offer of assistance, he warned, it could not "escape theresponsibility of what could amount...to crimes against humanity. Or, in the words of the Geneva Conventions, the failure to allow an available multinational force into East Timor would leave Indonesian leaders open to international prosecution because they had not taken "all feasible measures" to stop the violence.

Secretary-General Annan's comments are not themselves binding. The international community must still find ways to give them force of law. Yet his logic resonates precisely because it corresponds with the developing view that there is no sovereign prerogative to commit or sponsor crimes against humanity. He thus has pointed the way toward precluding the death-squad dodge.

If the Annan doctrine prevails, a government that claims to be unable to stop mass killing would have a criminally enforceable duty to invite a ready international force to lend a hand, at least so long as the force itself was committed to respecting human rights and humanitarian law. The incentive to commit atrocities by proxy would significantly diminish, and the barriers of sovereignty would no longer constrict the duty to prevent crimes against humanity.

Kosovo

The NATO bombardment triggered by atrocities in Kosovo was launched against the backdrop of Bosnia, where the international community had waited more than three long years before using decisive military force to halt genocide. Then, only the accumulated record of "ethnic cleansing"-the siege of Sarajevo, the slaughter of Srebrenica, the concentration camps, the rapes, the forced displacement-finally generated the political will to move beyond endless negotiation and appeasement, to transcend neutral humanitarianism, and to meet terror with significant force. The two-week bombing of military targets in Serb-held Bosnia territory in 1995 helped to end the bloodshed and produce the Dayton peace accord.

The international community's response in Kosovo reflected some lessons learned from Bosnia. Recognizing that Milosevic's method of fighting was to kill, rape and forcibly displace civilians, it acted this time soon after Yugoslav and Serbian troops began committing crimes against humanity. The massacres and forced displacement in 1998 and early 1999 were seen not as aberrations but as precursors of a larger round of ethnic slaughter. The deployment of the Kosovo Verification Mission (KVM) in October 1998 temporarily curtailed the violence and enabled hundreds of thousands of forcibly displaced Kosovar Albanians to return home before winter.

But Yugoslav and Serbian troops massed again in Kosovo in early 1999 and resumed their abusive ways. It was then that international negotiators finally stopped treating Milosevic as an essential guarantor of peace and insisted that NATO troops replace his forces in Kosovo and assume responsibility for law and order. Unlike East Timor, where economic pressure could be applied to secure Jakarta's consent, economic sanctions were already long in place against Yugoslavia stemming from its complicity in the Bosnian conflict. NATO was thus propelled more quickly to threaten military force to gain consent to the deployment of protective troops. To deny Yugoslav and Serbian troops the opportunity for Bosnia-style hostage taking as a way of deterring the use of force, the international community withdrew the unarmed KVM verifiers. Milosevic's continued intransigence led to a seventy-eight-day NATO bombing campaign, during which Yugoslav and Serbian forces murdered thousands, forcibly displaced hundreds of thousands, committed unknown numbers of rapes, and engaged in vast arson and destruction. The bombing campaign ended with the withdrawal of these forces from Kosovo, the deployment of international troops, and the return of the Kosovar Albanian refugees.

Military intervention might have been avoided altogether had the international community paid attention to Kosovo's plight during the preceding decade. The repression of Kosovo's ethnic Albanian population that followed the withdrawal of its autonomous status in 1989 sounded a clear but unheeded warning of trouble to come. But a world preoccupied by the conflict in Bosnia paid little attention to the largely peaceful protests of the Kosovar Albanians. Only with the emergence of the Kosovo Liberation Army and, given Milosevic's brutal history, the seemingly inevitable slide toward a ruthless counterinsurgency effort did the international community finally take note.

In addition, the international community's long misguided deference to Milosevic as a supposedly indispensable partner for peace in the Balkans, and its unwillingness to expose its troops to even modest risks in Bosnia, undermined the International Criminal Tribunal for the Former Yugoslavia's potential for deterrence. When Bosnian Serb political leader Radovan Karadzic and military leader Ratko Mladic were indicted for genocide, NATO troops refused to arrest them. To this day, Karadzic is believed frequently to sleep undisturbed within a stone's throw of French troops in Bosnia. Moreover, the major Western powers, particularly Washington, London and Paris, refused to give the tribunal the intelligence evidence it needed to indict Milosevic for command responsibility for the atrocities of "ethnic cleansing" committed in Bosnia and Croatia. The international community thus sent a message that it was not terribly serious about applying international justice to Serb leaders. That lesson could only have emboldened Milosevic to embark on a new round of slaughter in Kosovo.

Once the decision was made to use force against Yugoslavia, NATO's military conduct raised separate and serious concerns. Even granted Milosevic's long history of slaughter, his recent record in Kosovo of murder and forcible displacement, and his new massing of troops within Kosovo, NATO's bombing seemed to accelerate plans for large-scale ethnic killing and dislocation. Yet NATO was clearly unprepared for this turn of events. With political constraints standing in the way of the nonconsensual deployment of ground troops, NATO depended on aerial bombardment to stop the killing. But the strategic bombing campaign that it pursued focused to a large extent on factories, basic infrastructure, and other strategic targets throughout Yugoslavia, even when their connection to troops in Kosovo was remote. Particularly at first, relatively little attention was paid to halting Yugoslav and Serbian military activity in Kosovo. Moreover, NATO's extraordinary efforts to avoid casualties among its pilots precluded the low-flying aircraft that might have helped to identify and strike the attacking forces more accurately. NATO's strategic bombing campaign undoubtedly disrupted troop movements and ultimately was an element in inducing surrender, but its timetable was too slow and its focus too diffuse to stop the atrocities in Kosovo before months had passed. Despite their suffering, KosovarAlbanians generally applauded NATO's action, but the question remained whether these beneficiaries of the NATO campaign might have been assisted more directly and effectively.

Also disturbing is that NATO seemed to play fast and loose with the requirements of international humanitarian law. This law, largely codified in the widely ratified Geneva Conventions of 1949 and their Additional Protocols of 1977, is designed to spare noncombatants the hazards of war. NATO is bound by these basic rules whenever it goes to war. Particularly when it fights in the name of human rights, it should abide by these standards scrupulously.

Despite NATO's efforts to minimize civilian casualties, about 600 civilians were killed by NATO bombs, in some ninety incidents. Moroever, NATO sought to squeeze Yugoslavia's civilian population to pressure Milosevic to surrender. That rationale dangerously undermined the "principle of distinction" which requires that military attacks be directed against only military targets and not civilian objects. Many of the targets attacked-the electrical grid, heating plants, civilian broadcast facilities, bridges, refineries-disrupted civilian life in a way that was clearly "excessive in relation to the concrete and direct military advantage anticipated," the standard of proportionality codified in Article 57 of Protocol I to the Geneva Conventions. The destruction of some of these targets did not even make an "effective contribution to military action" or offer a "definite "definite military advantage," the baseline tests for a legitimate military target codified in Article 52 of Protocol I.

The result was a dangerous inversion of the principles of humanitarian action. In part to avoid risks to its troops, NATO did not seem to take the most rapid or effective steps to achieve the paramount humanitarian goal-stopping the slaughter of Kosovar Albanians. Yet the means it did employ chipped away at what should be a sharp distinction between military targets and civilian objects and thus increased the risks for all civilians in future conflicts. Destructive echos of this approach could already be seen in 1999 in Russia's attacks in Chechnya and Israel's attacks in Lebanon. Thus, while NATO's actions in Kosovo showed a heightened willingness to override sovereignty to stop crimes against humanity, they signaled a disturbing disregard for the principles of humanitarianism that should guide any such action.

The Critique of Military Intervention

The use of military force to prevent severe human rights crimes has given rise to a range of concerns. The importance oi scrupulously complying with international humanitarian law has already been noted. Another common concern is that military intervention might become a pretext for military adventures in pursuit of ulterior motives. Vigilance against such misuse of the human rights name is clearly warranted. Memories of the U.S. invasions of Grenada and Panama, for example, have not faded. But the interventions in East Timor and Kosovo gave fewer reasons for concern on this score than prior interventions.

In East Timor-where, as noted, economic and diplomatic pressure secured consent to military deployment-Western strategic concerns worked, if anything, against intervention.

The Western powers were hardly looking for an excuse to upset the world's fourth most populous nation, a growing economic force, and the dominant power in Southeast Asia-particularly, as noted, at a time of democratization and separatist tension. Nor was sympathy for East Timor's claim of self-determination decisive, since the international community had largely tolerated Indonesia's occupation of the region for more than two decades. There was concern for the credibility of the U.N., which had pledged to oversee a referendum process that was violently disrupted, and Australia may have feared an influx of refugees. But the primary motive for intervention seemed to be genuine public anxiety over the plight of the East Timorese people before the rampaging militia.

In Kosovo, NATO's concern for its credibility may have contributed to its decision to begin bombing when Milosevic rejected the Rambouillet peace proposal. Worries about large refugee flows destabilizing Macedonia's delicate ethnic mix, producing cascading instability in the Balkans, and ultimately seeking entrance to the rest of Europe may also have driven NATO to seek the return of Kosovar refugees once Yugoslav and Serbian troops began forcibly expelling them in large numbers upon commencement of the bombing. Yet the common denominator in the multinational consensus behind NATO's action was fundamentally humanitarian, including fear that Milosevic would extend the sweep of genocide to Yugoslavia's southern province. Whatever mixed motives might have guided NATO's action, the desire to stop crimes against humanity was clearly a major goal.

One way of minimizing the pretextual use of military intervention would be to insist that the U.N. Security Council always grant prior approval. But as it functions today, with the five permanent members free to exercise their vetoes for the most parochial reasons, the council cannot be counted on to authorize intervention even in dire circumstances. China and Russia seem preoccupied by perceived analogies to Tibet and Chechnya. The United States is sometimes paralyzed by an isolationist Congress and a risk-averse Pentagon. Britain and France have let commercial or cultural ties stand in the way. If the council cannot change its culture, it risks losing its moral authority before the widely felt imperative that something be done to save people from crimes against humanity.

Another way to limit the misuse of military intervention would be to develop criteria for when it should occur. For example, Human Rights Watch considers advocating nonconsensual military intervention only when it is the last feasible option to avoid genocide or comparable mass slaughter.

Governments might well adopt other criteria. But given the risk to life inherent in any military action, only the most severe threats to life should warrant consideration of an international military response. And even then, as noted, strict compliance with international humanitarian law should be imperative.

Some critics challenge humanitarian action in Kosovo and East Timor on the grounds of selectivity. Why intervene in these situations, they ask, and not in Angola or Colombia, in Chechnya or Sudan? Again, legitimate concerns with equity lie behind this objection. Yet, theworld should hardly deny a helping hand to people facing mass slaughter simply because it might not act to stop similar atrocities elsewhere.

Instead, the international community must address its troubling tendency to ignore atrocities in certain regions, particularly sub-Saharan Africa. Widespread atrocities in Angola, Burundi, the Democratic Republic of Congo, Sierra Leone, and Sudan, to cite but a few examples, received nowhere near the attention they deserved in 1999.

When confronted with this problem of inconsistency, the Western powers too often hide behind the excuse of regionalism. According to this view, governments will assume the risks involved in stopping crimes against humanity only for their neighbors. It is said to be only natural that NATO limit its intervention to Europe and that only Australia was willing to take the lead on East Timor. Yet this narrow view leaves responsibility for parts of the world with some of the worst atrocities to those least equipped economically and militarily to end them.

The atrocities in Sierra Leone, for example, were left to a Nigerian-led West African force, ECOMOG, with little Western assistance.

The U.S. government's proposed solution for Africa is the African Crisis Response Initiative, a U.S.-trained African force designed to provide a local emergency response capacity. But this idea has received only tepid support in Africa, including initial rejections by Nigeria and South Africa. And without deeper Western involvement, it is unlikely to have the capacity to confront Africa's numerous, highly abusive conflicts.

Given the world's tremendous disparities of wealth and power, governments with the greatest resources should not pretend to have met their humanitarian obligations by passing the buck to those with the least.

Not every human rights tragedy lends itself to military intervention. Indeed, Kosovo and East Timor may have been easier cases, because each had a colorable claim to self-determination and a local population that overwhelmingly favored intervention.

Before using military force to stop crimes against humanity, planners at minimum should be confident that intervention will not make matters worse, by provoking a wider war or setting in motion a string of new atrocities.

But if the use of military force to stop atrocities is to gain moral acceptance, those who initiate it must remain conscious of the desperate need for international assistance in parts of the world that are now mostly neglected. Victims of atrocities deserve effective assistance wherever they cry out for help.

The Emerging International System of Justice

The past year significantly reinforced the trend toward an international system of justice for the world's worst human rights offenders. The highlights of this trend were progress toward the extradition and prosecution of Pinochet, the indictment of Milosevic, advances in prosecuting those behind the Rwandan genocide, and the remarkable momentum toward the establishment of the International Criminal Court. Important issues of international justice also arose in Cambodia, Sierra Leone, and East Timor. The international justice system is still rudimentary, capable of ensnaring only an occasional tyrant. But the progress made in 1999 left the world a considerably smaller place for those who commit the most heinous human rights crimes. It symbolized a growing international commitment to justice as a means of showing respect for the victims of serious abuse, building the rule of law at the international level, and deterring tomorrow's would-be gross abusers of human rights. Like the use of military intervention, the emergence of an international system of justice signals that sovereignty is no longer the barrier it once was to action against crimes against humanity.

Pinochet

The October 1998 arrest of Chilean General Augusto Pinochet yielded several momentous rulings by the British courts.

Foremost was the definitive rejection of Pinochet's claim that, as a former head of state, he deserved immunity from prosecution. In a complicated decision in March 1999, the House of Lords reaffirmed an earlier ruling that Pinochet could be extradited to Spain for his role in torturing perceived political opponents. The Lords limited the scope of his prosecution to crimes that took place after December 1988, when Britain's ratification of the Convention against Torture took effect. Because many of Pinochet's abuses were committed a decade earlier, some feared that the ruling would preclude a courtroom accounting of his worst offenses. But a magistrate in October 1999 held that much of this material could be admitted into evidence, either to demonstrate a continuing conspiracy to commit torture that extended beyond December 1988, or to show the continuing mental torture of the families of victims whose earlier "disappearance" the military had never acknowledged.

Milosevic

If the Pinochet case represents the first international prosecution of a former head of state, the indictment of Milosevic by the International Criminal Tribunal for Former Yugoslavia was the first international attempt to prosecute a sitting head of state. This long-awaited indictment charges Milosevic with crimes against humanity committed by Yugoslav and Serbian troops under his command in Kosovo. Milosevic does not face immediate prosecution, since no one seriously proposes sending troops to Belgrade to arrest him. But there is reason to believe that he will see his day in court. The significant domestic opposition to his rule may succeed in replacing him, or he may find no feasible way to extend his term as Yugoslav president beyond the constitutionally mandated limit of mid-2001. The new government would then have a large incentive to surrender him for trial in the Hague, since many of Serbia's would-be international donors have made his surrender a condition for future non-humanitarian aid. Or, like the leader of the murderous Kurdish rebel organization, Abdullah Ocalan, who was bounced from country to country until his abduction by Turkish security forces in February 1999, Milosevic may find himself in perilous exile in a world that is increasingly unsympathetic to fugitive perpetrators of crimes against humanity.

Then-Chief Prosecutor Louise Arbour described the Milosevic indictment as the first "real-time" response to atrocities-a capacity she sought for the tribunal to maximize its deterrent effect. The tribunal's investigative response to the Kosovo crisis was still slower than it should have been, but the rapid-response goal is laudable. However, the tribunal's deterrent effect remains handicapped by Western ambivalence aboutapplying international justice to senior Serb leaders. Milosevic has still not been indicted for his role in Bosnia and Croatia, in large part because Western governments have not supplied the tribunal with the intelligence information it needs to prove his command responsibility. NATO's arrest of indicted Bosnian war crimes suspects has also been half-hearted.

In the first ten months of 1999, NATO troops arrested six indicted suspects in Bosnia, including Momir Talic, a top Bosnian Serb general who was deeply implicated in the Srebrenica savagery. But they allowed former Bosnian Serb military leader Ratko Mladic, who directed the barbarity at Srebrenica, to escape to Belgrade, and they continue to refuse to arrest former Bosnian Serb political leader Radovan Karadzic, who reportedly remains in Bosnia in an area controlled by French troops. NATO's timidity is due in part to its continuing preoccupation with avoiding risks to its troops and in part to its misguided belief that the arrest of Karadzic might destabilize Bosnia-a belief that, by undermining the tribunal's deterrent effect, led directly to the destabilization of Kosovo.

Trials for the Rwandan Genocide

The International Criminal Tribunal for Rwanda added a third panel of judges and permitted the consolidation of cases in an effort to expedite the trial of those accused of complicity in the 1994 genocide. During 1999, the tribunal found three suspects guilty of genocide, making a total of five convicted so far, including the former prime minister, Jean Kambanda. Those found guilty were sentenced to prison terms ranging from fifteen years to life. The tribunal also secured the arrest of five more former ministers in the genocidal government, increasing the number in custody to more than half of the cabinet at the time.

A Swiss military court also tried a Rwandan local official who had fled to Switzerland after Rwandan victims accused him of participating in the genocide. Although the panel of judges found that Swiss law did not permit the official to be charged with genocide or crimes against humanity, they convicted him of war crimes in violation of the Geneva Conventions and sentenced him to life in prison. In Belgium, an investigating judge has been preparing cases against others accused of genocide in Rwanda. These cases are expected to come to trial in early 2000.

The International Criminal Court

Burgeoning support in 1999 for the International Criminal Court (ICC) represented another pillar of the emerging international system of justice. By late October, eighty-nine governments have signed the Rome treaty to establish the ICC, many have begun the complicated process of revising domestic legislation to permit ratification of the treaty, and substantial progress has been made in drafting the court's rules of evidence and criminal procedure and the elements of the crimes it will prosecute. Several international organizations in 1999 also endorsed ratification, including the European Union, the Council of Europe's Parliamentary Assembly, the Commonwealth Law Ministers, the Inter-Parliamentary Union, and the Francophonie summit. It is now entirely foreseeable that within two or three years the treaty will have secured the sixty ratifications needed to establish the court.

The major sour note in this account remains the United States. Although the U.S. government has been a strong backer of international justice for other people, it continues to display hostility toward any international court like the ICC that even theoretically could apply to U.S. citizens. Once more, President Clinton has allowed the Pentagon's parochial views on the subject, backed by unilateralist sentiment in Congress, to determine U.S. policy on an issue of historic importance.

The ICC treaty already contains numerous safeguards, many proposed by the United States, to avoid unwarranted prosecutions. Yet the Pentagon seems satisfied with nothing short of an ironclad exemption for U.S. servicemen-an exemption that the rest of the world naturally finds to violate the ideal of universally applicable justice on which the court is founded. The treaty amendments favored by the Pentagon, such as an exemption for any act declared to have been officially authorized by the suspect's government, would upset the delicate consensus behind the Rome treaty and introduce a gaping loophole that the world's tyrants would eagerly exploit. The court's potential to punish oppressors, deter would-be despots, and bring a modicum of respect to the victims of heinous abuse would be undermined.

Washington's position is suffused with irony. To begin with, the Pentagon's professed inability to tolerate ICC jurisdiction is at odds with its military campaign over Kosovo. NATO's war with Yugoslavia, like its 1995 bombing of Serb-held sections of Bosnia, was subject to the jurisdiction of the International Criminal Tribunal for the Former Yugoslavia-a fact that seems not to have given the Pentagon much pause. Indeed, the Yugoslav tribunal has fewer safeguards against unwarranted prosecution than the ICC because the tribunal's jurisdiction is primary-it is empowered to supersede any national prosecution-while the ICC's jurisdiction is secondary-it must defer to any good-faith national prosecution.

In addition, given the many procedural safeguards in place, the best remaining way to protect against misuse of the ICC's powers would be to influence the culture in which these safeguards are applied. Yet the less engaged the U.S. government is with the court, the less influence it will have to shape that culture. The accelerating global enthusiasm for the court shows that the Pentagon's hope of "killing" it is delusional. There will be a court, and it will have jurisdiction over U.S. troops and commanders, whether Washington supports it or not. The sole open question is whether the United States will have any say in shaping the ethic by which the court exercises its powers. The Pentagon's rejection of the court, and hence of any direct influence over its evolution, ironically puts U.S. service members more rather than less at risk of prosecution.

Moreover, President Clinton's opposition to the ICC fuels the very isolationism that he has decried in the U.S. Congress. In October when the U.S. Senate rejected a treaty against nuclear testing, President Clinton spoke eloquently about the "new isolationism" that had infectedthe legislative branch. Others have described this approach as "armed unilateralism."

Either name refers to the parochial and misguided view that in an increasingly interconnected world, the United States might go it alone, that in a world in which ideas and economics are the dominant currency of power, the United States, with all its reluctance to risk the lives of its soldiers, might secure its place solely through military might. Yet President Clinton's failure of leadership-his deference to Pentagon obstructionism not only on the ICC but also on such issues as the treaty to ban landmines and the optional protocol to stop the use of child soldiers-serves only to reinforce this ostrich-like vision of the world.

Other Justice Issues

On two other occasions-in Sierra Leone and Cambodia-the U.N. took important though qualified stands against efforts to compromise international justice standards. In East Timor, its support of justice was more tepid.

In Cambodia, the collapse of the Khmer Rouge raised the possibility of prosecuting its leadership for its inhuman 1975-79 reign. Hun Sen, the current Cambodian prime minister, was willing to allow prosecutions, but sought to control them by keeping them subject to the highly manipulable Cambodian judiciary. Yet precisely because of the Cambodian judiciary's lack of independence, Hun Sen also needed an international imprimatur for the trials to be considered credible. As of late October, Kofi Annan had rightly refused to provide the U.N.'s seal of approval for any prosecutorial plans that fell below international due process standards.

The negotiations focused on the process for selecting a mix of international and Cambodian judges. Secretary-General Annan wisely insisted that, if the U.N. were to lend its name to the tribunal, the U.N. must choose the judges and prosecutor.

This was the only way of ensuring both that political considerations did not influence the selection of prosecutorial targets and that those people selected would receive a fair trial. Desirable as it would be to see the Khmer Rouge leadership in the dock, that should not occur at the expense of the high standards for independence and due process that the U.N. has set in the Rwandan and Yugoslav tribunals and the International Criminal Court. If the U.N. were to compromise these standards, it could expect other governments to insist on similar concessions. As of late October, discussions were ongoing between Cambodia and the U.N.

In Sierra Leone, the quest to hold highly abusive forces accountable was dealt an initial setback when the international community left the government of President Ahmad Tejan Kabbah no choice but to accept an amnesty for the perpetrators of unspeakable atrocities. The Revolutionary United Front (RUF), the rebel group headed by Foday Sankoh, killed tens of thousands, mutilated (usually by chopping off their limbs) thousands more, committed a range of sexual abuses and other atrocities, displaced hundreds of thousands, and wholly deserved prosecution. The U.N. High Commissioner for Human Rights, Mary Robinson, made an important contribution by visiting Sierra Leone and highlighting these atrocities.

Yet because the permanent members of the U.N. Security Council refused to pay the (U.S.) $1 million a day that it allegedly cost the primarily Nigerian troops of ECOMOG to protect Sierra Leone from the RUF, let alone to deploy U.N. peacekeepers, Nigeria threatened to withdraw its troops. The Kabbah government thus had no choice but to accept a peace accord that amnestied the RUF and offered its ruthless leaders a share of power. This impunity, and the failure promptly to deploy U.N. troops, encouraged new butchery and placed the Sierra Leonean people at tremendous risk.

A U.N. mediator played a disturbing role in brokering this agreement. Once that role was publicly challenged, Kofi Annan established an important precedent by ordering the mediator to add a reservation to the agreement indicating that the United Nations saw the amnesty as applying only to domestic and not to possible international prosecutorial efforts. Given the devastation in Sierra Leone, its national courts are probably incapable in any event of bringing prosecutions for some time. Even the proposed Truth and Reconciliation Commission, if it is ever created, may well find progress difficult. From the perspective of a broader timeline, international justice thus remains the only meaningful option. But the Security Council chose to ignore this issue in passing a subsequent resolution on Sierra Leone. It also failed to establish an international commission of inquiry-the usual prelude to an international criminal tribunal-as was done for East Timor. At best, the U.N.'s refusal formally to accept amnesty for those behind the RUF's executions and mutilations means that these killers risk Pinochet-like prosecutions whenever and wherever they might travel, or be expelled, abroad.

In the case of East Timor, the same international community that worked to press Indonesia to accept the Australian-led international forces in mid-September seemed reluctant to hold the Indonesian military accountable for the atrocities that triggered the need for this deployment.

The hesitation was apparently due to concern that too much pressure on the Indonesian army could backfire, even though Indonesian pro-democracy activists stressed that democratization could go forward only if the army were held accountable. On September 27, Asian countries as a bloc rejected or abstained from voting on a U.N. Commission on Human Rights resolution calling on the Secretary-General to set up an international commission inquiry into violations of humanitarian law in East Timor.

The U.S. government and the European Union approved the inquiry but only on the grounds that it cooperate with Indonesia's National Commission on Human Rights, a body respected in Jakarta but not trusted in East Timor. The resolution passed, but the international commission appointed was weak, and its departure for East Timor was subjected to politically motivated dithering. Questions of whether key countries, like the United States and Australia, would share intelligence with the commission, and whether a new government in Jakarta would cooperate with it, remained unresolved at the end of October.

Justice, Peace, and Democracy

The developments of 1999 provided new evidence for the longstanding debate about the effect of pursuing justice on efforts to secure peace or establish democracy. Some have argued that justice may have a detrimental effect because a leadership threatened with trial and punishment may be reluctant to stop fighting or permit a transition to democratic rule. In fact, the events of 1999 tend to show not only thatjustice can be pursued without these anticipated costs, but also that the quest for justice can sometimes enhance the search for peace and democracy.

Milosevic is Exhibit 1 for the case that justice facilitates, rather than impedes, peacemaking. Already at Dayton in 1995, Milosevic showed himself willing to accept a peace accord without insisting on amnesty from prosecution for his complicity in atrocities in Bosnia and Croatia. Moreover, the Yugoslav tribunal's indictment of Karadzic and Mladic had helped make the Dayton accord possible by marginalizing the Bosnian Serb political and military leaders. Again in 1999, the tribunal's indictment of Milosevic for crimes against humanity in Kosovo proved no obstacle to his acceptance of a peace plan for the province. Indeed, by establishing Milosevic as an international pariah, the indictment may have helped to delegitimize him before his people, weaken his grip on power, and thus push him toward accepting NATO's terms for peace.

Similarly, the prosecution of Pinochet, despite the fears of some, proved not to have disrupted democratization in Chile. To the contrary, more progress was made in 1999 in extending the rule of law to the Chilean military than in the decade since he relinquished the presidency. Until Pinochet's October 1998 arrest in London, no crime covered by his 1978 amnesty had been prosecuted. But Pinochet's arrest broke the military's aura of invincibility. Suddenly, the Chilean courts began exploiting a legal detour around the amnesty to launch prosecutions of various military leaders.

Because the official perpetrators of a forced "disappearance" have, by definition, not acknowledged the victim's fate, the courts can consider the crime ongoing-a kidnapping without an end. Even if the victim was seized and "disappeared" before the 1978 amnesty, the military's ongoing refusal to provide this critical acknowledgment-its refusal to settle questions about the victim's fate and allow family members to mourn their loss and move on with their lives-extends the crime beyond 1978 and the amnesty's protection. Dozens of cases are now pending in the Chilean courts under this theory, making it possible for the first time to say that the rule of law is beginning to extend to the Chilean military.

East Timor presents a more qualified but still interesting example. Although no international mechanism of justice has been established to address the militias' rampage, the United Nations did initiate an international commission of inquiry to investigate Jakarta's role in the violence. In Rwanda and Bosnia (though not yet in the Democratic Republic of Congo), such commissions were precursors to the establishment of an international criminal tribunal. The naming of a commission for East Timor did not prevent the Indonesian government from accepting the deployment of a multinational force for the territory. Nor did the army block the election of the first president in the forty years of Indonesian independence chosen in a ballot that did not have a predetermined outcome. As in Serbia and Chile, an international focus on the crimes of the military leadership seems to have shaken rather than entrenched its grip on power.

A Reinforced Public Morality

The progress made in 1999 in standing up to crimes against humanity represents more than a doctrinal qualification of the prerogatives of sovereignty. Behind the advances in international justice and the increased deployment of troops to stop atrocities lies an evolution in public morality. More than at any time in recent history, the people of the world today are unwilling to tolerate severe human rights abuses and insistent that something be done to stop them. This growing intolerance of inhumanity can hardly promise an end to the atrocities that have plagued so much of the twentieth century. Some situations will be too complex or difficult for easy outside influence. But this reinforced public morality does erect an obstacle that, at least in some cases, can prevent or stop these crimes and save lives.

A key catalyst of this strengthened public morality has been the human rights movement-the network of organizations that in recent decades has sprung up in nearly every country-and its ability to capture attention and support from the press and public. The movement gains its adherents from its ability to speak to the most basic values of people around the world. By carefully investigating abuses and holding them up for public scrutiny under international standards, it helps to build and reinforce public judgments that this conduct is wrong. By monitoring and exposing the international community's reaction to these abuses, it generates public demands that something be done to counteract the worst tendencies of humankind.

In some countries, human rights organizations have gained large numbers of members and supporters. The millions of Colombians who took to the streets in October to protest the country's highly abusive war is but one example. More often, the membership of these groups is modest. Yet their power is less in their numbers than in their ability to project their values into the public debate and to change public perceptions of what can and should be done to combat abuse. The Mine Ban Treaty, which entered into force on March 1, faster than any other multilateral treaty, is a good illustration; by the end of October, eighty-nine governments had ratified the treaty.

Most human rights work addresses abuses that have not risen to the level of crimes against humanity. Indeed, an important goal of the human rights movement is to stop abuses before they multiply, to identify and halt the discrimination and repression that can be a precursor of crimes against humanity. This day-to-day human rights work has helped to build a strong public belief that human rights violations of any sort are intolerable. The past year showed how strong this public morality has become even in difficult cases, when it forced the international community to intervene in Kosovo and East Timor despite the lack of strategic interest and the powerful considerations militating against intervention.

Of course, this public morality will not always be enough to move governments. Sometimes countervailing forces will be too formidable. Further work is needed to solidify public judgments so that governments feel obliged to respond to serious human rights abuse moreconsistently. But as the millennium closes, the human rights movement's ability to capture and marshal the ideals of humanity makes it possible to hope for a future of greater respect for human life and the inherent dignity of each human being.

Human Rights Defenders

Despite the unmistakable progress made in standing up to the most severe abuses, the struggle to defend human rights remains a difficult and, at times, deadly battle. Each year we note with sadness our colleagues who gave their lives for the cause of human rights. Between November 1998 and October 1999, ten human rights defenders and two of their family members were murdered in circumstances that suggest they were killed because of their work. Three of the murdered human rights defenders were in Colombia, while one defender and his two sons were murdered by Serbian police in Kosovo.

In Antioquia, Colombia, Julio González and Everardo de Jesús Puerta, who worked for the Committee of Solidarity with Political Prisoners (Comité de Solidaridad con los Presos Políticos, CSPP), were forced off a public bus in July and shot by presumed paramilitaries. Colombian paramilitaries frequently act with the acquiescence if not active support of the Colombian army. In May, anthropologist and University of Antioquia professor Hernán Henao was also killed by three intruders who broke into a faculty meeting. Professor Henao, a human rights activist, had served as director of the Institute of Regional Studies (Instituto de Estudios Regionales, INER), a research center for the study of political conflict and community development. Darío Betancourt, a social scientist at Colombia's National Teaching University (Universidad Pedagógica Nacional) who ran a think tank on political violence, was forcibly "disappeared" in April. His body was found the following September in Bogotá, showing signs that he had been executed.

In Kosovo, Serbian police came to the home of Bajram Kelmendi in March and beat him in the presence of his family. The police then took away Kelmendi, an Albanian human rights lawyer, and his two sons, Kastriot and Kushtrim.

The police refused to give Kelmendi's wife, Nekibe, who is also a human rights lawyer, information on the whereabouts of her husband and sons, telling her that she should "ask NATO." The next day the bodies of the three men were found in a gas station outside Pristina. They had been shot dead. Bajram Kelmendi had defended many political prisoners in Kosovo and, shortly before his death, had taken up the defense of an Albanian-language newspaper that the police had closed.

In Northern Ireland, human rights lawyer Rosemary Nelson was killed in March by a car bomb a short distance from her home, not far from the school attended by one of her three children. Throughout the 1990s, Rosemary Nelson had frequently represented suspects accused of politically motivated offenses. Her clients were typically arrested under emergency laws, held in specially designed holding centers, and interviewed without access to an attorney. Nelson had frequently been the target of harassment, death threats, and intimidation, including threats on several occasions by members of the Royal Ulster Constabulary (RUC).

In Uzbekistan, Akhmadhon Turakhonov, a member of the Independent Human Rights Organization of Uzbekistan (IHROU), died in prison in June after being deprived of adequate medical care. Turakhonov, who had been in detention since late December 1998, was serving a six-year prison term for "attempted overthrow of the state" for his public criticism of the government.

Russia lost one of its leading human rights activists and anti-corruption campaigners in November 1998 when Duma deputy Galina Starovoitova was murdered near her St.Petersburg home. At the time of this writing, law enforcement agencies say that they are still investigating her killing.

In Sri Lanka, Neelan Tiruchelvam was assassinated in July by a suicide bomber believed to have been sent by the Liberation Tigers of Tamil Eelam (LTTE). Neelan Tiruchelvam was an internationally respected human rights leader who had founded both the International Centre for Ethnic Studies and the Law and Society Trust, a human rights research and advocacy organization. As a Tamil member of parliament, Tiruchelvam had angered the LTTE by proposing an alternative to a separate Tamil state.

In Cambodia, Pourng Tong, 55, a volunteer for the Cambodian Human Rights and Development Association (known by its acronym, ADHOC), was killed in his home in Kandal province on December 19, 1998. He had been helping villagers resist evictions. A bodyguard for a company attempting to carry out the evictions allegedly shot Tong half a dozen times with an assault rifle. As of October, no one had been arrested for the murder.

6

Special Issues in Human Rights

Academic Freedom

Academics in dozens of countries in 1998 were harassed, censored, dismissed, beaten, or imprisoned for peacefully expressing their ideas. Although governments increasingly recognized the importance of universities in promoting technological and economic progress, many continued to take aggressive measures to restrict the scope of expression and inquiry on campus. Respect for academic freedom and the basic civil and political rights of academics thus continued to be a sensitive barometer of free expression worldwide.

International human rights standards offer academics a principled basis for resisting authoritarian political pressures and defending the institutional autonomy necessary for academic excellence. Freedom of expression, defined in international treaties as "freedom to seek, receive and impart information and ideas of all kinds, regardless of frontiers," is a precondition of academic freedom. A university fulfills its mission when academics are not forced to support an official line, an economic agenda, or a political ideology, but rather are free to use their talents to advance human knowledge and understanding. Although international attention to the right to free expression understandably has emphasized artistic freedom and freedom of the press, essential attributes of an open, democratic society, institutions of higher education have played a critical role in preserving and giving meaning to the right. Abuses tracked by Human Rights Watch in 1998 illustrated the often fragile status of the right to free expression on university campuses. Academics were most often targeted when they publicly criticized government authorities, were active in opposition movements or citizens groups, or investigated subjects deemed "politically sensitive" by the authorities. Reprisals against such professors, researchers, and students included harassment, censorship, arbitrary dismissal and expulsion, and, in the worst cases, imprisonment and torture. Although such reprisals most obviously violated the civil and political rights of the academics concerned, they also directly undermined academic freedom. Academics do not exist in a social or political vacuum, and participation in public affairs and contributions to public debate are important aspects of the academic mission.

The most dramatic campus developments took place in Serbia, where universities were subjected to de facto takeover by the ruling parties, and in Indonesia, where students and faculty, defying decades-old restrictions on the campus community, emerged at the forefront of a nationwide movement for political reform. Developments in Belarus, Burma, China, Cuba, Egypt, Ethiopia, Jordan, Malaysia, and Uzbekistan further demonstrated the range and continued prevalence of government efforts to rein in critical inquiry and expression by academics in 1998.

Serbia

On May 26, 1998, under pressure from Yugoslav President

Milosevic, the Serbian parliament passed a law that deprived faculty members throughout Serbia of their longstanding right to participate in the selection of rectors, faculty deans, and governing boards, and that effectively canceled—subject to renegotiation—the contracts of all professors and other teaching staff. Because the assault on the universities coincided with a crackdown on the independent media, coalitions of faculty that formed to protest the law had difficulty getting their message to the Serbian public. Demonstrations opposing the new law were violently suppressed. As the conflict in Kosovo intensified and Serbian nationalist rhetoric grew more strident, the pressures on critics of the new university law mounted.

The most dramatic changes under the new law took place at the University of Belgrade, which had long been a center of student protest and continued to be home to a number of prominent faculty critics of the government. At least sixteen faculty deans there were replaced shortly after the law took effect. Twelve were forcibly removed and four resigned in protest. Fifteen of the sixteen newly appointed deans were members of the ruling parties. None of the replaced deans were members of political parties.

At least thirteen influential politicians in Serbia's ruling coalition—comprised of Milosevic's Socialist Party of Serbia (SPS), the Yugoslav Left (JUL, a party led by Mira Markovic, Milosevic's wife), and the Serbian Radical Party (SRS, led by Serbian Deputy Prime Minister and ultranationalist Vojislav Seselj)—were named to the governing and supervisory boards of the University of Belgrade and its component faculties. Another high-ranking member of JUL, Jagos Puric, was appointed rector.

The first professor to be fired under the new law was Dr. Vladimir Vodinelic, a law professor and one of Yugoslavia's leading civil law theorists and one of sixteen professors in the Faculty of Law who had signed a declaration opposing the new law. Two weeks later, twelve law professors who had protested Vodinelic's firing were suspended. In the Faculty of Philology, the new dean, Radmilo Marojevic (a member of the SRS), declared that his faculty was not doing "useful work," announced his intention to close the World Literature Department, and moved to transfer thirty academics who had refused to sign new contracts to lower paying positions. Professors in other faculties, including philosophy and electrical engineering, also came under assault from the politically appointed deans.

One of the stated aims of the drafters of the law was the "depoliticization" of the universities. At the time the new law was enacted, officials emphasized that higher education in Serbia had become inefficient because faculty were spending too much of their time engaging in opposition political activities. A more ominous rationale for the new law was articulated by new philology dean Marojevic: "Sadly, our country and our culture are somehow under occupation from within. We have a fifth column in scholarship, in culture, everywhere." Marojevic praised the law as a "good attempt to return to Serbian character, [to bring] a national, cultural,and authentic character to this university."

Academic excellence requires that decisions affecting teaching, scholarship, and research be made on the basis of academic merit, not political favoritism or ideological litmus tests. The danger of the new law was that such decisions were put into the hands of government-appointed officials, with no participation by independent faculty members. The new law removed existing safeguards for academic autonomy, opening the door to political meddling in academic affairs by both present and future governments of Serbia. In principle, the university should be an institution open to all on the basis of merit, an important intellectual resource not only to governments and industry, but also to individuals and interests independent of the state. The University Act, however, appeared to be turning universities in Serbia into institutions that exclusively served the interests of Serbian state authorities.

Indonesia

Developments in Indonesia in 1998 contrasted sharply with those in Serbia. In Indonesia, a nationwide student protest movement played an instrumental role in forcing the resignation of President Soeharto and in opening the door to democratic reform. Students and faculty emerged at the forefront of the reform movement in large measure because they publicly spoke their minds, courageously and consistently ignoring regulations banning campus political expression and activity, as well as other laws, regulations, decrees, and abusive practices that had long limited political and intellectual freedom on Indonesia's campuses and in Indonesian society.

The transformation began in January 1998, when the collapse of Indonesia's currency was greeted by an outpouring of demands for an end to Soeharto's thirty-two-year rule. In early March, when opposition leaders failed to mount any significant challenge to Soeharto and Indonesia's compliant and largely hand-picked parliament unanimously elected Soeharto for a seventh five-year term, the student protest movement became the nationwide focus of opposition to Soeharto.

The movement was not confined to campus radicals, but involved literally hundreds of thousands of students from hundreds of institutions, including private universities, academies, and institutes as well as leading public universities and state teacher training and Islamic institutes. The students were actively supported by many faculty, alumni, and university administrators. At a rally held during the last week in April at Dr. Soetomo University in Surabaya, for example, Poncol Marjada, the university rector, read a statement formally calling on students to participate in the demonstrations to express their concerns. At a rally at Gadjah Mada University in Yogyakarta the same week, senior professor Dr. Loekman Soetrisno declared to the crowd of students: "If Martin Luther King could trigger the birth of a new America, you, too, the young people, can create a new Indonesia." The protests reached a climax in May, when students increasingly were joined by non-academics at rallies. Soeharto resigned on May 21 after security forces shot and killed four student protesters at Trisakti University in Jakarta on May 12, and in the wake of mass rioting in several cities which followed the killings and left more than 1,000 people dead.

President Soeharto's "New Order" government had not been uniformly hostile to the academic community. Many academics and students backed Soeharto when he first assumed power, and the government's emphasis on rapid economic growth created opportunities for a range of academic specialists. As Soeharto consolidated his power, however, he eventually turned his attention on the universities, which were emerging as a leading source of opposition to the policies of the new government. By the early 1980s, political controls over academic life in Indonesia were among the most intrusive in the world. Incoming academics were subjected to mandatory political background checks, students were subjected to compulsory on-campus ideological indoctrination sessions, students and academics who directly challenged the government were prominent among Indonesian dissidents imprisoned for exercising their basic rights, and political expression and activity were expressly outlawed on campus through a policy that the government called "Normalization of Campus Life." In addition, a wide range of publications was censored, speakers were barred from campus by police and military authorities, seminars were monitored and subject to cancellation at the discretion of the authorities, and academic research was stymied by labyrinthine state research permit issuance procedures.

In the last years of Soeharto's rule, mounting pressures for greater political openness and respect for citizen's rights in Indonesia led to a number of concessions by the government. The government's relaxation of controls, where it occurred, however, was not accompanied by formal repeal of regulations legitimating the government's intrusive policies or by the implementation of institutional protections for basic rights. The result was continuing uncertainty about the boundaries of the permissible. This uncertainty, together with periodic government crackdowns on dissent and intimidation of those who delved into matters that the government viewed as sensitive, created a climate hostile to intellectual innovation and vigorous debate. The lack of clear boundaries also created a black market in ideas, a continued gap between what people said in private and what they were willing to say in public, depriving the society of the intellectual dynamism that results from open expression of competing viewpoints.

Although significant institutional and legal barriers to freedom of expression remained in place in Indonesia after Soeharto's resignation, the reform movement opened the door to more wide-ranging public debate in Indonesia. The changed climate was evident as early as April 1998 when Soeharto's minister of education, Wiranto Arismunandar, invoked the twenty-year-old "Normalization of Campus Life" regulations in an effort to quell the mounting campus protest movement. Arismunandar's remarks immediately became the subject of heated media debate. His invocation of the repressive campus regulations was roundly criticized in the press and his warning was completely ignored in practice by students and their faculty supporters. Subsequent efforts to control the protests—including attempts to portray the student movement as infiltrated by communist agitators, the abduction and forced disappearance of more than two dozen political organizers by groups within the military, and a nationwide ban on public protest marches by students—did nothing to stop the protests and indeed sparked an indignant counterresponse.

After Soeharto's ouster, the country continued to face daunting challenges, including government corruption and nepotism, social unrest fueled by a steadily worsening economic crisis, an entrenched military with a prominent role in politics, a history of militaryatrocities in such places as East Timor, Aceh, and Irian Jaya, and deep-rooted ethnic hostility directed against Indonesians of Chinese ancestry. For the first time, however, these issues were being discussed openly. Scholars and students, well-situated to explore the social and political realities that underlie such problems and help in the search for solutions, were prominent among those participating in the discussions.

Reprisals against Dissenting Academics

Although developments in Serbia and Indonesia provided the most dramatic illustrations of the intimate connection between academic freedom and protections for basic rights, activist professors, researchers, and students were targets of government repression in a wide range of countries. Due to the high public profile of universities and of the academics who were involved, such attacks often played an exemplary role, serving as a warning to individuals throughout society that dissent and political opposition would not be tolerated.

In Cuba, professor Felix A. Bonne Carcasses, economists Marta B. Roque Cabello and Vladimiro Roca Antunez, and attorney Rene Gomez Manzano were imprisoned throughout 1998 for their membership in an opposition group and for publicly insisting that greater democratization was a prerequisite to effective economic liberalization. In Ethiopia, the government continued to imprison Dr. Taye Wolde Semayet, a former professor and president of the Ethiopian Teachers' Association (ETA), which had emerged as a leading critic of the government's policies. From July to September, Dr. Taye was shackled twenty-four hours a day. Although the government initially had alleged that Dr. Taye was involved with terrorist attacks on the government, the most serious charges against him were dropped for lack of evidence and the remaining charges related solely to Dr. Taye's alleged association with a proscribed organization, charges which he vehemently denies.

In Malaysia, students at a number of universities were harassed and some were suspended in September 1998 for joining peaceful rallies in support of deposed Deputy Prime Minister Anwar Ibrahim. The Malaysian University Act forbids students from participating in opposition politics. In September, Education Minister Datuk Seri NajibTun Razak announced that the ministry was monitoring students involved in Anwar's "reformasi" or reform movement, the general objective of which was to reduce corruption in government. Student supporters from the Mara Institute of Technology (IT) were threatened with expulsion and blacklisting from government educational institutions for being involved in Anwar's campaigns. Six students of Universiti Utara Malaysia were arrested and subsequently suspended for involvement in political activity related to a September parliamentary by-election.

In Uzbekistan, dozens of students were expelled from state institutions of higher education for wearing Islamic attire. In May, the government adopted a repressive law on religious organizations that, among its provisions, prohibited the wearing of "ritual" dress in public. Under the law, viewed by critics as an attempt to marginalize religious groups perceived as a potential source of political opposition to President Islam Karimov, female students who wore the hijab (Muslim clothing usually including a head scarf and a long robe) were expelled and male students with beards were subjected to pressure to shave or else were expelled.

The National Security Service (SNB) followed several expelled university students who had met with Human Rights Watch and warned them not to speak with foreigners. The expulsion of students for religious dress in Uzbekistan was the mirror image of policies pursued in Iran after the 1979 revolution and in Sudan in the early 1990s, where students and professors have been expelled or dismissed for failing to demonstrate "proper" religious comportment.

In Belarus, Human Rights Watch documented seven cases of politically motivated dismissals, warnings, and expulsions of academics that formed part of a broader government crackdown on independent political expression. One case was that of Liubov Lunyova, a human rights activist who prior to her dismissal had worked as a lecturer on a fixed-term contract in the history department at the Belarusian State University (BGU) in Minsk.

Although Lunyova was told by university officials that she was let go because of lack of funds, she was fired shortly after Belarussian President Lukashenka had publicly berated the university rector for keeping activist teachers on staff. Lunyova told Human Rights Watch, moreover, that despite the alleged lack of funds, new lecturers had been hired after her dismissal. When Lunyova sought a job at another school, the director of the school told her that he "would be fired within half an hour" if he gave her a job.

Censorship and Ideological Controls

In China, continuing Communist Party control of the universities was strengthened with new legislation in August 1998 giving campus-based party officers the power to override administrative decisions made by university presidents. Scheduled to take effect in January 1999, the law also gave campus-based party committees responsibility for "enforcing the policies and guidelines of the Communist Party and...work related to political, ideological and moral education."

In Malaysia, after reports began circulating in late 1997 of the adverse public health consequences of the dense haze that was then enveloping much of the country from uncontrolled forest fires in Indonesia, the government issued a decree requiring that all researchers investigating the subject have their work screened and preapproved by "higher authorities." In Egypt, the government successfully pressured officials at the American University (AU) in Cairo to censor the book Muhammad , a classic text by the internationally renowned scholar, Maxime Rodinson. The book had been available in Egypt since the 1970s and was included on a course syllabus in 1998. After a prominent Cairo journalist published an article alleging that the book contained passages that insulted Islamic beliefs, President Mubarek, through the minister of education, ordered AU to ban the book. In response to the president's order AU administrators informed professors that they could no longer include the book in their reading lists and ordered it removed from the library and the campus bookstore.

In Jordan, the government enacted a broad new press and publications law giving government authorities broad powers of censorship. Among the requirements of the law was that universities and scientific research centers obtain prior permission from the Ministry of Information before importing potentially controversial books and writings. The new law also imposed onerousrequirements on independent research centers, including a provision forbidding such institutes and their employees from "receiving any financial assistance or support from any non-Jordanian party" and providing for steep fines and closure for up to six months of any institute that violated the policy.

Crackdowns on Student Protest

In many countries, governments responded to student protests with violent crackdowns and at times the indiscriminate use of force against protesters. In Indonesia, the Soeharto government's nationwide ban on public marches by students early in the year backfired when violent clashes between students and hundreds of police and troops massed at campus gates added fuel to an already developing, nationwide political crisis. In countries including Kenya, Zimbabwe, and Nigeria, governments used school closures as a weapon to stop demonstrations and penalize students for expression of their political views.

Government suppression of student protest continued to be extreme in Burma, where most universities remained closed throughout 1998, the country's intellectual resources and institutions paralyzed. Universities in Burma had been closed for seven of the ten years since the 1988 pro-democracy uprising was crushed by the army. The closures in 1998 dated from December 1996, when the government shut down the universities following major campus rallies protesting police violence against students.

Freedom Of Expression On The Internet

Despite growing acknowledgment during 1998 among

governments around the world that the Internet promotes participation in civil and political life within countries and beyond, legislative proposals continued to threaten free speech on the Internet. While dissidents in authoritarian countries continued to take risks using the Internet to seek help and information, regulators in these parts of the world were quick to refine screening and other controlling technologies. As a result, in a half-dozen countries, Internet access providers (including public libraries) were implementing filtering technologies and other voluntary measures to make prior censorship of on-line communications a reality. The trend is towards extending these technologies more broadly, with global implications for free expression. On-line content providers may soon be forced to start rating their content; those failing to rate their content may find their material blocked from public access. As local rating criteria are used to define ratings, the danger is that these restrictive criteria will limit the diversity of expression on the Internet, where content is as diverse as human thought.

In October 1997 the European Parliament had consented, in principle, to the use of filtering and screening devices. Subsequently the European Commission requested to the European Parliament to foster research into technical issues, in particular filtering, rating, and tracing techniques, taking into account Europe's cultural and linguistic diversity. Ironically, authoritarian regimes around theworld were soon to implement these techniques and principles to restrict free expression on the Internet.

For example, Singapore's National Internet Advisory Committee (NIAC) in its September 1998 report recommended that the local industry be required to label Web sites using PIÇS (Platform for Internet Content Selection)- compliant content rating classification systems, such as that developed by the Recreational Software Advisory Council (RSAC).

Implementing this would mean that unrated sites would be automatically blocked. Even if this system were only adopted in Singapore, all unrated Web sites around the world would be blocked when the system was used.

Saudis expected to get local access to the Internet by the end of 1998. But the King Abdulaziz City for Science and Technology (KACST), which was to act as the kingdom's gateway to the Internet, set up firewalls that would block access to sites considered sensitive. In anticipation of the new service, Council of Ministers Decision 163 required parties using the Internet to refrain from "any activities violating the social, cultural, political, media, economic, and religious values of the Kingdom" and prohibited sending or receiving coded information without prior authorization.

Bahraini authorities apparently continued to block access to some Web sites, including that of the London-based Bahrain Freedom Movement, and to seek ways to improve the government's capacity to monitor political speech on the Internet. Jalal Alawi Sharif, a Batelco engineer who was arrested in March 1997 reportedly on the grounds that he was transmitting information to the BFM via the Internet, remained in detention without charge or trial as of September 1998.

In mid-January, public hearings were held on a draft Thai Internet Law. Its submission to Cabinet was then delayed due to a lack of "public acceptance" arising out of its potential impact on freedom of expression. During August the Royal Thai Police department's "Internet Police" proposal demanded that the Telephone Organization of Thailand (TOT) implement caller-ID features for all local Internet Service Providers. Caller-ID would be used to gather information about each user logging onto the network, including the telephone numbers they used, their login names and the times of the day they connected and disconnected.

During 1998 China encouraged Internet use while restricting the flow of overseas information. The new Internet regulations replaced interim regulations restricting the free flow of information. The regulations spelled out in greater detail the responsibilities, procedures and penalties for various players involved in Internet communication. During July, China arrested and charged a software engineer with subversion for supplying e-mail addresses to a U.S.-based pro-democracy magazine and Web site known as "Big Reference". According to the Information Center of Human Rights and Democratic Movement in China, Shanghai's cyber-police force was reinforced with 150 additional computer experts. An example of the activism that would be affected by such controls was the Septermber 28 issuance, by a small group of dissidents, of a challenge to the government in the form of two manifestos on freedom and social justice. The two declarations in English translation were posted on the sites of a group in New York, Human Rights in China and an international group, the Digital Freedom Network and in faxed copies.

On August 11, Malaysian police arrested a man and a woman and accused them of false reporting about riots in the capital, spread by an Internet newsgroup. They were tracked down with the help of Malaysian Institute of Microelectronic Systems (MIMOS), which provides sole access to the Internet in that country. On August 13 Malaysian police detained a third suspect. All three were held under the Internal Security Act (ISA), which allows detention without trial for sixty days. On September 24, the suspects were charged in the magistrate's court under Section 505 (b) of the penal code, which carries face a maximum sentence of two years in prison. On September 28 Tengku Azzman, chairman and chief executive officer of MIMOS, was quoted by the government news agency Bernama saying that the government had no intention of practicing Internet censorship.

In October 1997 the South Korean government blocked access to the GeoCities on-line community (based in the U.S.) because of a site that espouses North Korean beliefs.

In June 1998 a Turkish court sentenced a teenager, Emre Ersoz, to ten months suspended jail time for making comments about the police while participating in a daily on-line forum, hosted on local Internet provider Turknet. He reportedly had criticized rough police treatment of a group of blind people who were protesting against potholes in pavement in the nation's capital, Ankara.

Even G-7 governments were found rushing to regulate the Internet before people understand its full potential as a tool of citizen participation.

For example, during 1998 Britain continued its attempts to persuade the other E.U. countries to adopt an e-mail interception system providing unconditional government access to e-mails, arguing that this was essential to fight cross-border crime. A September 1998 report by the U.K. Department of Trade and Industry acknowledged the need for radical rethinking while developing regulation for the information age.

Despite such announcements, however, the government continued working on plans to allow the police to tap electronic communications to combat on-line crime. British law enforcement agencies continued to demand that Internet Service Providers (ISPs) reveal all sorts of information about users. Such disclosure had the potential to include interception of e-mail messages without legal due process, a serious violation of privacy.

The Russian state police proposed a plan to monitor every piece of data sent over the Internet within Russia's boundaries. Proposed amendments to the mass media law which were discussed in the Russian Duma in March 1998 included a clause suggesting that any publisher of electronic information should register with and obtain a license from the government.

A Bavarian court convicted Felix Somm, former head of the German division of the U.S. on-line service provider Compuserve, in May 1998, of spreading child pornography and other illegal material by providing access to such information on the Internet.

Germany's new multimedia law stipulated that access providers are not generally liable for Internet content, although they are required to take reasonable measures to block access to banned material. In June, a twenty-five-year-old university student in Berlin was charged for maintaining an Internet home page that provided an electronic link the left-wing newspaper Radikal.

In the United States, Australia, France, Spain and the U.K, legislative proposals contemplated establishing controls on access to and use of cryptography, or data-scrambling technology, which is used to protect the privacy of communications on-line. The insistence of Britain and France forced the European Commission, in September 1998, to water down its plan to protectInternet privacy using the encryption software.

Countries like Australia and the U.S. led an international push to restrict access and use of encryption software. Human Rights Watch, along with other members of the Global Internet Liberty Campaign (GILC), attempted to counter this effort through defining standards for on-line privacy protection and cryptography based on international human rights law. The current push for restricted access to cryptography may make the use of freely available software like PGP illegal or impossible for human rights groups from developing countries and in the long term even by nongovernmental groups in the most developed countries.

Recognizing that the Internet can be a democratizing force and a useful tool for the advocacy of human rights, during 1998 Human Rights Watch extensively used its World Wide Web site for campaigns on human rights violations in several regions and promoted other global issues including campaigns to end recruitment of child soldiers, to establish the International Criminal Court, and for ratification of the 1997 treaty banning landmines. While continuing to document and protest attempts to silence the Internet, we expanded our on-line advocacy and campaigning work in coalition with civil liberties, women's, labor, journalists' and other groups internationally to promote participation in civil and political life.

A website which contains a host of important and relevant information on the subject of freedom of expression on the internet is the Global Internet Liberty Campaign (GILC) website

7

Policy on Discrimination Against Older Persons

The Ontario Human Rights Code states that it is public policy in Ontario to recognize the inherent dignity and worth of every person and to provide for equal rights and opportunities without discrimination. The provisions of the Code are aimed at creating a climate of understanding and mutual respect for the dignity and worth of each person, so that each person feels a part of the community and feels able to contribute to the community.

The Code prohibits discrimination because of age in the social areas of employment, services, goods, facilities, housing, contracts and membership in trade and vocational associations. The Code's protection against age discrimination extends to all persons over the age of 18, except in the case of employment discrimination where persons are protected from age discrimination only until age 64.

Most of the complaints filed with the Ontario Human Rights Commission (the "Commission") regarding age discrimination are in the area of employment with services constituting the next largest area. Complaints in which age is cited as a ground of discrimination account for approximately 7-9% of the Commission's case load.However, it is likely that incidents of age discrimination, particularly in job seeking and in services such as health care, remain unreported.

This policy is the outcome of extensive research and consultation on issues of discrimination faced by older persons in Ontario. In 2000, the Commission published a Discussion Paper, Discrimination and Age: Human Rights Issues Facing Older Persons in Ontario which set the stage for a province-wide public consultation.In June 2001, the Commission released its Consultation Report, Time For Action: Advancing Human Rights for Older Ontarians ("Time for Action").

The Report was intended to be a broad examination of all issues that may have an impact on the dignity and worth of older adults and may affect the enjoyment of equal rights and opportunities. As such, it contained a number of recommendations for government and community action. The Commission also outlined several measures that it would take to address age discrimination, including developing this public policy statement.

Several conclusions resulted from the Commission's research and consultation and form the basis of this policy:

- Age discrimination is not seen as something that is as serious as other forms of discrimination despite the fact that it can have the same economic, social and psychological impact as any other form of discrimination.
- Society has accepted age-based criteria as a way in which to structure policies and programs and to make decisions about people in areas such as employment and services.
- Despite the fact that the population is aging, many aspects of society have been designed in a way that is not inclusive of older persons.

- Preconceived notions, myths and stereotypes about the aging process and older persons persist and give rise to discriminatory treatment.
- Age often works in "intersection" or combination with other grounds of discrimination to produce unique forms of disadvantage. For example, women experience aging differently than men and older persons with disabilities face compounded disadvantage.
- Employers, service providers and others with responsibilities under the Code are looking for more information and guidance on meeting their human rights obligations vis-à-vis older persons. A shortage of skilled workers in certain fields means creative strategies are being sought by employers to attract and retain older workers.

This policy sets out the Commission's position on discrimination against older persons as it relates to the provisions of the Code. It deals only with issues that fall within the Commission's jurisdiction and which can form the subject matter of a complaint to the Commission.

Time for Action contains a broader examination of social policy and other issues which must be addressed through positive action by government and community partners. In addition, the Commission is engaged in, and will continue to undertake, initiatives to address broader human rights issues related to age. The purpose of this policy is to:

- help the public understand how the Code protects persons against discrimination as they age;
- make older persons aware of their right to equal treatment in employment, housing accommodation, goods, services, and facilities, contracts and membership in trade unions, without discrimination;

- assist employers and providers of services and housing accommodation, to understand their responsibilities under the Code;
- set out how the Commission and its staff will deal with complaints based on age; and
- provide a resource for educational initiatives and development of internal policies and procedures.

Commission policy statements set standards for how individuals, employers, service providers and policy makers should act to ensure compliance with the Code. They are important because the public has the right to expect that the Commission will deal with cases in a way that is consistent with its published policies. While they are not binding on the human rights board of inquiry or on courts, they are often given great deference, applied to the facts of the case before the court or tribunal and even quoted in the decisions of these bodies.

The analysis and examples used in this policy are based on the Commission's research on age discrimination, principles and recommendations developed by the United Nations to guide countries in the promotion of the rights of older persons, cases that have come before the Commission, tribunal and court decisions and the input of individuals and organizations in the Commission's consultation process.

"Age", "Older" Person and Human Rights Concepts

The Definition of "Age" in the Human Rights CodeSubsection 10(1) of the Code defines age as follows:

"age" means an age that is eighteen years or more, except in subsection 5(1) where "age" means an age that is eighteen years or more and less than sixty-five years.

Subsection 5(1) is the section that prohibits discrimination in employment. This means that the Commission cannot receive a complaint of age discrimination in employment from someone who is 65 or older. The Commission cannot amend the Code. Until the Ontario Legislature amends this definition of "age", it is not contrary to the Code for employers to require employees to retire at age 65 (or older) and employees cannot challenge this practice. Similarly, workers who remain employed past age 65 cannot complain if their employer treats them differently (e.g. in remuneration, benefits, hours, vacation etc.) because of their age. There is no upper age limit on the right to be free from harassment on the basis of age. Therefore, workers age 65 or over can file age harassment complaints with the Commission.

As the Commission is not empowered to receive a complaint about age discrimination in employment experienced by persons age 65 or over, this policy does not deal with the issue of mandatory retirement at age 65. In Time for Action, the Commission recommended to the Legislature that the Code be amended to eliminate the blanket defence to mandatory retirement at age 65 and to extend protection against age discrimination to workers aged 65 or older. The Commission is still awaiting a decision on this recommendation.

Persons who are 65 or older can bring a complaint of age discrimination in all social areas other than employment, including:

- services, goods and facilities (health care, social services, transportation services, shops, restaurants, education etc.)
- housing accommodation (such as rental accommodation, condominium facilities, hotels and motels, residential care facilities and social housing);
- contracts; and

- membership in occupational associations, trade unions and self-governing professions.

The Terms "Older" and "Ageism" as Used in this Policy

Persons may experience age discrimination at any time in their lives. However, persons who belong to, or are perceived to belong to, certain age groups tend to be more vulnerable to certain forms of discrimination. For example, younger persons may be more likely than middle-aged or older persons to be turned away from housing because of stereotypes around the desirability of younger tenants. As this policy focuses on the forms of age discrimination most commonly experienced by persons as they age, it has become necessary for the Commission to adopt some terminology to describe the cohort who is at risk for experiencing these forms of age discrimination. It has chosen to do so by using the term "older" persons or workers. However, discrimination on the basis of age can be experienced by persons beginning as early as 40 to 45, particularly in employment. The term "older" is not meant to denote "old age" or stigmatise persons in any way. Rather it is simply being used as a relative concept, meaning older than those who are less likely to face the particular types of discrimination being discussed.

It is important to remember that the concept of who is an "older" person may be a contextual one. For example, while older workers are generally those over age 45, if the average age in a workplace is 25, a 37 year old job applicant may be turned away because of a perception that she is unable to fit in with the workplace culture. Therefore in some situations, for example where the allegation pertains to negative attitudes and stereotypes about aging, it may be necessary to think not in terms of absolute, but rather relative age. In other contexts, actual age may be relevant, for example, where a person's age is used to determine eligibility for a program or service.

The terms ageism and age discrimination are both used in the Commission's work. Ageism refers to a socially constructed way of thinking about older persons based on negative stereotypes about aging as well as a tendency to structure society as though everyone is young. Ageism refers primarily to attitudinal barriers while age discrimination encompasses actions, namely treating someone in an unequal fashion due to age. Moreover, discrimination is a legal concept that has been defined in the Code and in court decisions and not every manifestation of ageism is age discrimination within the meaning of human rights law and policy. Ageism, however, is often the cause of age discrimination. It is therefore important from a human rights perspective to address both acts of age discrimination and also ageist attitudes that exist in society.

Other Human Rights Concepts Referenced in this Policy

The Code and human rights case law contain a number of complex concepts and legal standards. For those who are not familiar with the terminology, it can be very difficult to understand a discussion of rights issues when these terms are used.

The Intersection of Age with Other Grounds of Discrimination

The experience of age discrimination may differ based on other components of a person's identity. For example, certain groups of older persons may experience unique barriers as a result of the intersection of age with gender, disability, sexual orientation, race, ethnicity, religion, culture and language.

This understanding of the complexity of how people experience age discrimination means that, where appropriate to the circumstances of the alleged discrimination, all relevant grounds must be considered along with age.

Example: A 55-year-old woman alleges that she was refused a job as a waitress because she didn't fit the image that the restaurant is trying to promote.

The evidence reveals that the restaurant employs many younger women as waitresses as well as older men as waiters and maître d's. The fact that older persons (men) are employed and younger women are employed does not necessarily defeat her claim of discrimination as there may be unique stereotypes attributed to older women with regard to image or attractiveness.

It may be necessary to examine any stereotypes as well as the historical, social and political context associated with the particular combination of grounds.

Example: A 72-year-old man has recently immigrated to Canada. He has difficulty finding a physician in his community as there is already a shortage of doctors and he is perceived as a patient who will require a lot of time due to his age and the fact that he is not conversant in English or French.He finds he must attend drop-in clinics and when he complains of feeling depressed, he is told that it is to be expected considering his age and the fact that he has recently moved to Canada. He is not sent for further assessment.

In some cases persons may be put at a 'double disadvantage' as a result of age combined with other grounds of discrimination.

Example: Empirical evidence confirms that older persons and persons with disabilities all face higher unemployment rates. As well, members of "visible minority" groups are more likely to be underemployed. Therefore, an older African Canadian person who is developing a disability will likely face compounded disadvantage in a job search.

As a society, we must be aware of the unique ways in which people may experience disadvantage. In seeking to understand rights and responsibilities, in addition to this policy dealing with age discrimination, where other grounds of discrimination may be at play, other Commission policies such as the Policy and Guidelines on Disability and the Duty to Accommodate may be relevant.

General Principles

When is Differential Treatment Discriminatory?

The purpose of anti-discrimination laws is to prevent the violation of human dignity and freedom through the imposition of disadvantage, stereotyping, or political or social prejudice.

In many cases, differential treatment because of age will clearly be discriminatory. However, in other cases, it may be necessary to consider whether the treatment can be said to constitute "discrimination" in the sense of being something that is protected by human rights law.

Some age-based criteria or qualifications are not based on stereotypes, are not offensive to human dignity and do not target a historically disadvantaged age group.

For example, discounts on services for persons under 25 or over 55, retirement schemes that are based on a minimum age combined with years of service and measures aimed at facilitating the transition from full-time employment to retirement would not likely be considered discrimination within the meaning of human rights law and policy.

In the context of equality claims under s. 15 of the Canadian Charter of Rights and Freedoms (the "Charter"), the Supreme Court of Canada has offered the following three broad inquiries as a tool for determining whether discrimination has occurred:

(1) *Differential Treatment*: Was there substantively differential treatment, either because of a distinction, exclusion or preference, or because of a failure to take into account the individual's already disadvantaged position within Canadian society?

(2) *An Enumerated Ground*: Was the differential treatment based on an enumerated ground, in this case age?

(3) *Discrimination in a Substantive Sense*: Finally, does the differential treatment discriminate by imposing a burden upon, or withholding a benefit from, an individual? The discrimination might be based on stereotypes of a presumed group or personal characteristics, or might perpetuate or promote the view that an individual is less capable or worthy of recognition or value as a human being or as a member of Canadian society who is equally deserving of concern, respect and consideration. Does the differential treatment amount to discrimination because it makes distinctions that are offensive to human dignity?

In Law v. Canada (Minister of Employment and Immigration) the Supreme Court of Canada applied these three inquiries to conclude that even though the claimant was not entitled to a survivor's pension when her spouse died simply because of her age (she was 30), it was not discrimination under s. 15 of the Charter. Under the pension scheme, full benefits were paid to surviving spouses over the age of 45, partial benefits were paid to those between 35 and 45 and no benefits were available to surviving spouses under age 35. The Court found that persons under age 45 have not historically been subjected to discrimination and that younger persons do not face the same barriers to long-term labour force participation that the benefit was designed to address. The law did not stereotype, exclude, devalue or demean adults of the claimant's age.

Age 65 Benefits, Special Programs and Special Interest Organizations

In certain circumstances, the Code permits programs and benefits aimed at a specific age group.

The Code expressly provides for the preference of persons over 65 years of age:15. A right under Part I to non-discrimination because of age is not infringed where an age of sixty-five years or over is a requirement, qualification or consideration for preferential treatment.

This permits seniors' discounts, seniors-only housing and other benefits aimed only at persons over 65.

As well, section 14 of the Code permits the use of special programs in all social areas. This allows preferential treatment or programs aimed only at older persons, even if they have not yet reached the age of 65, if the purpose of the program is to relieve hardship or economic disadvantage or to assist disadvantaged persons or groups to achieve equal opportunity.

It is important that special programs be designed so that restrictions within the program, for example with regard to the age of those eligible to participate, are rationally connected to the objective of the program. A failure to do so, can lead to successful challenge of the program and a finding that it is discriminatory.

The Commission's Guidelines on Special Programs provide detailed information on how a special program can be planned, designed and monitored.

Section 18 of the Code allows certain types of organizations to limit participation or membership based on Code grounds including age:18.

The rights under Part I to equal treatment with respect to services and facilities, with or without accommodation, are not infringed where membership or participation in a religious, philanthropic, educational, fraternal or social institution or organization that is primarily engaged in serving the interests of persons identified by a prohibited ground of discrimination is restricted to persons who are similarly identified.

Example: A charitable organization that is primarily engaged in serving the interests of women over the age of 55 through researching issues of interest to this group and lobbying government to make changes to law and policy limits its membership to persons similarly identified.

An organization that wishes to rely on this defence must show it meets all of the requirements of this section.

When are Standards, Factors, Requirements or Rules that Discriminate on the Basis of Age Justifiable?

A person who wishes to assert a human rights complaint (a "complainant") has the burden of making out a prima facie case of discrimination. After that, the legal burden shifts to the party complained about (often known as the "respondent") to justify that its action is reasonable and bona fide in the circumstances (rules that can be justified as bona fide are often referred to as bona fide requirements or BFRs.).

Section 11 of the Code allows a respondent to justify a standard, factor, requirement or rule that has an adverse effect because of age by showing that it is a BFR.

For example, a requirement that job applicants be "recent graduates" of a program may have the effect of excluding older candidates who are less likely to have completed their studies recently. However, the employer has the opportunity to show a justifiable reason for this requirement.

Section 24 allows direct discrimination in employment for reasons of age if the age of the applicant is a BFR because of the nature of the employment. For example, if an employer has a policy of hiring persons under a certain age only, it can attempt to show that this is reasonable in the circumstances.

Whether the discrimination is direct or by adverse effect, the Supreme Court of Canada has set out the same three-step test for determining whether discriminatory standard, factor, requirement or rule can be justified as a BFR. The respondent must establish on a balance of probabilities that the standard, factor, requirement or rule:

was adopted for a purpose or goal that is rationally connected to the function being performed,

was adopted in good faith, in the belief that it is necessary for the fulfilment of the purpose or goal, and

is reasonably necessary to accomplish its purpose or goal, in the sense that it is impossible to accommodate the claimant without undue hardship.

The ultimate issue is whether the person who seeks to justify the discriminatory standard, factor, requirement or rule has shown that accommodation has been incorporated into the standard up to the point of undue hardship.

In this analysis, the procedure used to assess and achieve accommodation is as important as the substantive content of accommodation. The following non-exhaustive factors should be considered in the course of the analysis:

- whether the person responsible for accommodation investigated alternative approaches that do not have a discriminatory effect;
- reasons why viable alternatives were not implemented;
- ability to have differing standards that reflect group or individual differences and capabilities;
- whether persons responsible for accommodation can meet their legitimate objectives in a less discriminatory manner;
- whether the standard is properly designed to ensure the desired qualification is met without placing undue burden on those to whom it applies; and
- whether other parties who are obliged to assist in the search for accommodation have fulfilled their roles.

Combating "Ageism" Through Inclusive Design

The Commission has defined "ageism" to mean, in part, "a tendency to structure society based on an assumption that everyone is young, thereby failing to respond appropriately to the real needs of older persons." Ageism occurs when planning and design choices do not reflect the circumstances of all age groups to the greatest extent possible.

The Supreme Court of Canada has recently made it clear that society must be designed to be inclusive of all persons. It is no longer acceptable to structure systems in a way that assumes that everyone is young and then to try to accommodate those who do not fit the mould.

Rather, the age diversity that exists in society should be reflected in the design stages so that physical, attitudinal and systemic barriers are not created.

As a corollary to the notion that barriers should be prevented at the design stage through inclusive design, where systems and structures already exist, organizations should be aware of the possibility of systemic barriers and actively seek to identify and remove them.

Individualization vs. Assumption

Another emerging human rights principle that has particular significance for age discrimination is the notion of individualized assessment and accommodation.

In the past, many standards, factors, requirements and qualifications that discriminate on the basis of age have been justified on the basis of presumed characteristics associated with aging.

Example: Mandatory retirement of police officers and firefighters at age 60 has been accepted where an employer has provided evidence of cardiovascular disease and decline of aerobic capacity associated with aging and has shown that individualized testing is "impractical".

However, in light of recent decisions from the Supreme Court of Canada, the Ontario Court of Appeal and the British Columbia Court of Appeal it does not appear that this type of approach is sufficient.

Rather, those seeking to justify age based policies must show that individualized assessment as a form of accommodation is impossible, i.e. there is no method to do so, or that it represents an undue hardship.

The onus is on those seeking to justify a discriminatory standard to show they have provided individualized assessment and accommodation that recognizes the 'unique capabilities' of every individual, unless to do so would cause undue hardship.

Specifically, rather than judging individuals against presumed group characteristics, individualized assessment or testing to determine whether a person has the necessary aptitude or qualifications necessary should be used, subject to the undue hardship standard.

Employment

Assumptions and stereotypes about older workers are unfortunately all too prevalent in our workplaces. Older workers are often unfairly perceived as less productive, less committed to their jobs, not dynamic or innovative, unreceptive to change, unable to be trained or costly to the organization due to health problems and higher salaries. These ideas about older workers are simply myths that are not borne out by evidence. In fact, there is significant evidence that older workers:

- are highly-productive, boasting considerable on-the-job experience;
- do as well or better than younger workers on creativity, flexibility, information processing, accident rates, absenteeism and turnover;
- can learn as well as younger workers with appropriate training methods and environments; and
- do not fear change but rather fear discrimination.

Aging is a highly individual experience and it is not possible to generalize about the skills and abilities of a person based on his or her chronological age, any more than it is possible to make assumptions about someone based on any Code ground.

As a general principle, older workers should be treated as individuals, assessed on their own merits instead of presumed group characteristics, and offered the same opportunities as everyone else in hiring, training and promotion. They should be subjected to the same performance management practices as every other worker. Age, including assumptions based on stereotypes about age, should not be a factor in decisions about lay-off or termination.

In fact, underestimating the capabilities of older workers and treating them differently as a result can actually hinder them from maintaining their productivity and value. On the other hand, treating older workers equally allows employers to utilize a valuable resource, especially given that there are current and projected labour shortages.

Example: An employer assumes that an older worker is too difficult to train and, in any event, is "riding it out to retirement". She is not sent for training and is given performance reviews that do not meaningfully identify strengths and areas where there is room for improvement. Her skills do not remain current, she cannot work on improving in her weaker areas and she is less motivated to work hard because she feels she is not a valued worker, is not expected to perform and will never be recognized for her contribution.

Hiring

Older workers face significant barriers in finding employment. These can take the form of overt discrimination, such as not hiring someone simply because of his or her age, or more subtle or systemic discrimination, such as eliminating someone because of a perception he or she lacks "career potential". Such barriers can be compounded for persons who belong to groups that face their own barriers in accessing employment such as "visible minorities", newcomers to Canada and persons with disabilities.

Whether the discrimination is overt or systemic, the Code protects individuals against discrimination on the basis of age in the hiring process. The Code prohibits a job advertisement that directly or indirectly classifies or indicates qualifications by age (subsection 23(1)).

Similarly, application forms and oral questions must not directly or indirectly classify or indicate qualifications on the basis of age (subsection 23(2)). However, during an employment interview, questions may be asked about age provided that drawing a distinction on the basis of age is permitted under the Code.

This means that:

- In an advertisement: Statements that directly or indirectly relate to age should be avoided. Nothing should unfairly prevent or discourage an older worker from applying for a job. Requirements or duties for employment should be reasonable, genuine and directly related to the performance of the job.
- On an application form: While a form may ask "Are you 18 years or older and less than 65 years of age?", it should not ask any other questions about or relating to age or date of birth. The form should not request copies of documents that indicate age. Some employers may even choose not to ask when schooling was completed as this may often indicate age.
- During an interview: Questions relating to age should only be asked if a Code defence applies such as where a special program is in place (section 14), employment is aimed specifically at persons 65 or over (section 15), the employer is a special interest organization serving a particular age group (section 18), or age is a BFR.

Where age or date of birth is relevant to company pension and benefit plans, this information should be collected after making an offer of employment and should be kept confidential.

Demonstrating that age was directly or indirectly a factor in a hiring decision can be challenging. Employers rarely state that age was the reason for not giving an applicant the job. However, the following considerations may suggest that age was a factor in not hiring an applicant:

- The employer indicated qualifications at any stage of the recruitment process which can reasonably interpreted as a euphemism for age: e.g. "Do you think you can handle this job? It takes a person who is full of vim and vigour.", "We are looking to rejuvenate the workforce."
- There is evidence the assessor made an issue about the age of the applicant such as by commenting on the applicant's appearance and/or health or suggesting that the applicant may not fit into a youthful work culture.
- There is evidence that the employer considered age to be relevant when determining whether a person might adapt to certain job conditions such as menial tasks, minimal responsibility, low pay, shift work, being supervised by a younger person or that the employer felt that the candidate would not be trainable.
- There is evidence that the employer felt that person would be too costly to the organization because of his or her age: e.g. there was an assumption that there will be less time to recoup training costs, the applicant will expect a higher salary, or an older person will cost more in benefits, especially related to disability.
- There is a pattern in the past hiring or employment practices of the employer suggesting a preference for, or an institutional bias toward, younger workers. Statistical evidence can be relevant in this regard
- The applicant's qualifications for the job were as good or better than those of the person hired and the person hired was significantly younger than the applicant. This will be compounded if any of the above factors are also present,

such as a pattern of preferring younger applicants or commentary related to age. Also, the intersection of other disadvantaging factors such as race, ethnic origin, gender and disability may be important to consider if there is evidence of other patterns of discrimination in the workplace.

Some of the reasons that may be given for not selecting an older candidate are neutral on their face and yet may have a disproportionate impact on older persons. Some non-exhaustive examples include:

Turning away someone due to a perceived lack of "career potential": This requirement tends to adversely impact on older applicants, especially where they are applying for "entry-level" type jobs. Given the high rates of turnover in today's labour force and the fact that it is rare for someone to remain with the same organization for their entire career, it may be difficult to justify turning away an otherwise qualified person on the basis that they will not stay and grow within the organization solely because of their age.

Refusing an applicant who has "too much experience" or who is "overqualified": Sometimes this is simply used as a pretext for direct discrimination. However, most often this is a neutral factor that is not intended to discriminate. Nevertheless, turning away candidates who are "overqualified" may sometimes have an adverse effect on older persons, as they are more likely to have significant work experience and at the same time be changing careers due to a period of unemployment or a desire to transition into retirement. This can be compounded for others such as newcomers to Canada who may have no choice but to apply to positions they may seem overqualified for in order to get "Canadian experience" or to "get their foot in the door". Human rights law is based on the principle that employment decisions should be based on the applicant's

> ability to do the job. Therefore, the potential for human rights claims can arise where a qualified person is willing to take a job at the rank and salary offered but is refused simply because he or she has additional experience or skills.
>
> Eliminating an applicant because the applicant's background is too diversified or contains gaps, the applicant is too specialized and will have trouble learning or the applicant's experience is too remote: All of these factors can serve to disproportionately screen out older workers. Persons with longer work careers may appear more diversified and less "focused". This can be a particular problem for older women who have re-entered the workforce after childrearing and have had to retrain. Older workers may seem too specialized if they have been doing a job for a long period of time. Of course, if someone's experience is not relevant to the job, they may not be qualified and will not have to be hired. However, an older applicant should be attributed with just as much potential for redevelopment in a new area as a younger one. Finally, because older persons on average take longer to find a job and may have to accept aiternative employment, it will not be unusual for an older applicant not to have worked in his preferred occupation for some time. This should not be an automatic disqualifying factor. Rather, consideration should be given to whether the time lapse has devalued his credentials.

An employer can always demonstrate a non-discriminatory reason for not hiring a candidate or preferring another candidate. Therefore, it is a sound practice, both from a human resources and human rights perspective, to develop up-front, objective and job-related screening criteria for job competitions, to score candidates relative to these criteria and to retain all records related to job competitions for at least six months after the competition has been completed. As well, as discussed earlier in this policy an employer can disqualify someone because of age, either directly or through a neutral rule that has an adverse impact, if it can justify the requirement as reasonable and bona fide using the three-step test set out above. However, it should be borne in mind that the decisions to date where employers have tried to justify turning someone away solely because of their age have shown that it can be very hard to do so, especially if the concern for the employee's capacity is largely based on cost rather than on health and safety.

On-the-Job

Due to current and anticipated labour shortages, many employers, economists and labour market specialists are beginning to stress the importance of promoting retention of older workers. Of course, ensuring an equal opportunity and discrimination-free work environment is one of the best ways to ensure that older workers will remain in the workforce longer.

Subject to bona fide requirements, denying or restricting employment opportunities or treating a worker differently because of age is a violation of the Code. Examples of unequal treatment because of age include but are not limited to:

- Limiting or withholding employment opportunities including transfer, promotion and training opportunities;
- Not assigning an older worker to certain tasks or projects or subjecting an older worker to an unwanted transfer because of age.
- Performance managing older workers in a different way than other workers. This includes subjecting an older worker's performance to a higher level of scrutiny but also failing to performance manage because of a perception that

the older worker's performance is linked to age or because of a belief that performance management is not necessary as the person will soon be retiring.

- Not recalling someone from lay-off because of age.
- Terminating someone's employment because of age.

Of course, employers are not precluded from terminating older workers, using the same performance management criteria as for any other worker, where there are legitimate performance concerns that are based on objective evidence about the employee's ability to perform the duties of the job.

Statistical evidence regarding systemic issues in the workplace can constitute circumstantial evidence from which it can be inferred that discrimination probably occurred in an individual case.

Example: An organization was concerned about the aging of its employees and the fact that there would be a number of managers retiring within a 15-year period. Accordingly, recruitment practices were modified to meet the "long-term professional needs of the department." Statistical evidence dealing with age distribution of employees showed a disproportionate number of employees under 40 and the vast majority of recruits under 30.

The tribunal found that the organization had set about recruiting a younger work force and that the 43-year-old complainant who had been with the organization 7 years was not offered a promotion into a particular position, in part, because he did not fit the profile for the organization's recruits into that position. There was "compelling circumstantial evidence of an organizational predisposition against promoting older internal candidates into ES positions."

Older workers tend to experience disproportionate displacement or disadvantage as a result of workplace reorganization and downsizing. This can occur for a number of reasons such as an assumption that due to their age, or the fact that they have been doing their job a certain way for a period of time, they will have more trouble learning new technology or procedures, a perception that they will not be willing to accept changes to terms and conditions of work such as reduced pay or different work hours, or a belief that it is more equitable to displace them as they can take early retirement. As well, reorganization and downsizing may simply be used as a means to "rejuvenate" the workforce by getting rid of older workers.

Example: Due to an economic downturn, a company was forced to lay off staff. The complainant, a foreman, had worked for the company for over 32 years and was 57 at the time he was selected for termination along with another foreman who was aged 56. Both were offered a generous retirement package. The two foremen who remained were younger than the two released. The vice-president had prepared a note indicating that the two older workers who were terminated were told of the need to reduce people and that they "hoped to keep people with career potential". The tribunal found age discrimination on the basis of the good employment record of the complainant, the ages of those selected for lay-off compared to those retained and this statement which was found to be a "euphemism; its meaning concerns age."

Example: A business that served the public opened a larger facility designed to handle a greater volume of clients and introduced a new computer system. Two female staff persons in their 50s were transferred to positions which represented a demotion. Younger workers staffed the positions that they previously held. In finding age discrimination, the tribunal noted that the employer had not provided the complainants a meaningful opportunity to demonstrate they were able to perform the new duties, failed to provide even a minimal training and didn't give the complainants notice of the alleged performance concerns that were raised as a defence at the hearing. The tribunal noted that the employer's belief about older workers' capacity to learn and adapt to technological change was impressionistic and not a valid reason for changing the complainants' duties.

The following factors will help guide any consideration of whether age discrimination has occurred in a workplace reorganization or downsizing:

- Comparison of the performance of those who were selected for termination versus those who remained with the organization.
- Statistical evidence indicating a disproportionate number of younger workers can suggest an organizational bias for younger workers. As well, an analysis of the ages of those who were selected for adverse treatment in a reorganization as well as an analysis of the ages of those who were not can be relevant circumstantial evidence that age was a factor in the company's decision making.
- Criteria that tend to have a disproportionate impact on older workers such as: flexibility, rate of pay, ability to adapt to change, ability to be trained, being a generalist vs. a specialist. An assessment of personal suitability that is based on subjective considerations is always vulnerable to scrutiny as it can result in stereotyping or unconscious biases being brought into play.
- Indications that workers were selected for termination because of a perceived propensity to retire or because they are pension-eligible.
- A determination that the organization deviated from a previous approach, such as using seniority.
- Evidence of statements that can be interpreted as euphemisms for age such as "career potential", "rejuvenate", "renewal" etc.

On the other hand, there are ways in which employers can ensure that the decisions made in a workplace reorganization will be fair and non-discriminatory. Criteria should be objective and not based on subjective impressions about the particular worker's enthusiasm, flexibility or willingness to adapt. They should be demonstrably related to the goals of the reorganization or the needs that have been identified by the company. Ideally, positions rather than people should be selected for elimination and those positions should not subsequently be refilled.

Example: A company decides that due to decreased profits and the need to be more competitive in the marketplace, it will introduce a new, more automated production system. It identifies the number of positions that will be required to be staffed and what the duties of each will be. It also identifies the current positions that will no longer be required and why. It advises each person whose position has been determined redundant of this fact and how this decision was reached. It then invites all of these persons to compete for the new positions. It runs the competition using objective, age-neutral criteria and a scoring system which measures each candidate against the stated criteria. Past performance reviews are taken into account. The candidates with the best scores are selected and sent for training.

Retirement

Early retirement packages are often offered as an incentive to promote voluntary exit from the workforce. This can have many benefits to all workers: older workers may be offered a lucrative incentive which will allow them to pursue other interests or ambitions while at the same time ensuring that fewer workers will involuntarily lose their jobs. When designed properly, early retirement schemes are appropriate and will not raise human rights concerns. Also, if an employer has a non-discriminatory reason for terminating an older worker and wishes to offer the option of early retirement, there is nothing to prevent it from doing so. However, as early retirement schemes by definition target older workers, great care must be employed in using them as a means to achieve downsizing objectives.

In some situations using early retirement to encourage older workers to leave the organization can raise concerns from a human rights perspective. This will occur if there is direct or implicit pressure being applied to accept retirement. Furthermore, if the older worker does not accept retirement, is subsequently selected for termination and the reason for selecting him or her for termination is related to age, an organization may face a human rights complaint.

Example: A company decides that it needs to reduce its workforce by 10%. Human resources reviews the files of all workers and identifies all workers over the age of 60. Each one of them is called in for a meeting with management and told that they are nearing retirement age and should accept an early retirement package so that younger persons won't lose their jobs.

They are warned that if they do not do so, their position may be selected for elimination in which case they will simply receive severance and lose the opportunity to receive the early retirement package. Under these circumstances, some older workers feel compelled to accept the offer despite the fact that they were planning to work longer.

The fact that a generous retirement package is offered does not defeat a claim of age discrimination if the early retirement option was not truly voluntary.

Employers can take steps to ensure that an offer of early retirement is not coercive:

Define the eligibility criteria for the voluntary retirement program and share them with all staff, irrespective of age, through a neutral medium such as a written document. A response deadline and contact who can provide information should be provided so that those who qualify and are interested in the option can then decide if they wish to follow up on the offer, without any pressure from management. Some employers even chose to offer similar voluntary exit incentive packages to persons who are not near retirement age.

- Do not make any link between acceptance of the package and job loss. If the workforce is being downsized, indicate what the criteria will be for selecting the jobs that will be eliminated. Employees can even be assured that eligibility for the voluntary exit program will no way influence decisions about job loss.

Conversely, an employee cannot claim age discrimination if the employer does not offer him or her access to the voluntary exit program because the employer still requires his or her services.

In some occupations, employers may wish to impose mandatory retirement on workers who reach a certain age (of less than 65) on the basis that being less than that age is a BFR. For example, policies that require police officers and fire fighters to retire at age 60 are frequently used. In the past, before the new three-step test, such policies were found justifiable on the basis of evidence of a correlation between age and physical decline that could impact upon the ability to perform the essential duties of the job safely, combined with evidence that individualized testing is impractical. However, it should be noted that in light of the new three-step test articulated by the Supreme Court of Canada, it is no longer acceptable to rely on presumed group characteristics associated with aging. An employer seeking to justify mandatory retirement at an age less than 65 must show that individualized assessment, as a form of accommodation, is impossible, in the sense that there is no method to do so, or that individualized assessment represents an undue hardship. Moreover, the British Columbia Court of Appeal has recently confirmed that mandatory retirement policies should be approached on a case-by-case basis with the employer bearing the onus of establishing that its policy is justifiable in the circumstances of its workplace.

Finally, due to the definition of "age" in the Code, the Commission cannot receive complaints of age discrimination from those required to retire at age 65. Nevertheless, the Commission would encourage employers and unions to reconsider the utility and necessity of requiring employees to retire at age 65 and would encourage retirement policies that promote flexibility and choice

Pensions, Benefits and Seniority

The protections in the Code extend to pension plans. Such plans take effect once persons reach a certain age and are, therefore, of particular concern to older persons. As well, other grounds of discrimination such as disability, martial status and same-sex partnership status are often relevant when considering pension benefits.

Issues associated with pensions and benefits are often complex as they are governed by a complex statutory regime as well as actuarial factors. Complaints of discrimination in pension and benefit schemes must be considered on a case-by-case basis. In addition to the ability to justify a pension regime as a BFR, and the fact that some distinctions within pension and benefit plans may not be discriminatory within the meaning of human rights law, section 25 of the Code contains specific rules for pension and benefit plans. For example, subsection

25(2) of the Code provides that the right to equal treatment in employment is not infringed by an employee superannuation or pension plan or fund or a contract of group insurance between an insurer and an employer that complies with the Employment Standards Act and its regulations.

Sick leave plans that make benefits available based on age have been found to be discriminatory. Reduced pension benefits for early retirees have been found not to be discriminatory where the actuarial present value of reduced pensions for early retirees is at least equal to the present value of the deferred pension for those who wait until the age of eligibility for full pensions. Similarly, basing eligibility for pension benefits on reaching a certain age will not likely be considered discriminatory.

It is not permissible to use age to assign seniority when more than one employee is hired on the same day.

Accommodating the Older Worker

Older workers may require accommodation for reasons such as disability and the need to care for an ailing spouse or same-sex partner. The Commission's Policy and Guidelines on Disability and the Duty to Accommodate outlines rights and responsibilities with regard to accommodating workers with disabilities. In addition, the Commission's publication Human Rights at Work explains that an employer's duty to accommodate on the basis of family status, martial status and same-sex partnership status extends to employees who have work-related absences due to family-related responsibilities and encourages flexible work arrangements to help employees balance work and personal life. These obligations exist regardless of the age of the employee, however, due to a relationship between age and disability, these needs may become more apparent as workers, and members of their family, age.

Flexible work arrangements also benefit older workers who may be experiencing a decline in capacity and provide for an easier transition into retirement.

Traditionally, workforce participation has been seen as an 'all or nothing proposition'; people either work full-time or are retired. However, moving from fulltime work, spanning a lifetime, to the complete absence of work is a major change carrying with it social, psychological and financial implications.

In order to facilitate the transition from employment to retirement and to encourage older workers to remain in the workforce longer, there is currently a trend towards more flexibility and phased in retirement. Therefore, employers may want to consider measures such as:

- flexible hours and conditions of work such as compressed work weeks (working longer days in exchange for a shorter work week), flex-time (flexibility in start, end and break times as long as an agreed upon number of hours are worked), tele-working (working from home);
- part-time arrangements and job sharing, which allow for a transition into retirement while at the same time providing opportunities for other workers, e.g. a new parent who wishes to work part-time as well; and
- employing workers who have chosen to retire on short-term contracts or as consultants.

As discussed earlier, the duty to accommodate requires designing a workplace that is inclusive of older workers. It also requires individualized assessment and accommodation to meet the changing needs and capacities of older workers. For example, if an older worker finds a physically demanding task challenging, the employer should either assign it to someone else if it is not part one of the essential duties of the position, or seek other ways in which to accommodate the worker.

Housing Accommodation

Section 2 of the Code protects older persons against discrimination in housing. Housing includes a range of accommodation options including rental accommodation, condominiums, retirement homes and care facilities. There can be some overlap between housing and services, for example seniors' residences in which services such as housekeeping, meals or medical assistance are provided.

The Code prohibits either direct or adverse effect discrimination in housing. For example, a housing provider should not turn away older persons because it wishes to attract more youthful residents. Similarly, older persons who may be paying lower rents due to longer tenure in their rental unit should not be targeted for eviction by landlords who wish to attract new tenants at a higher rent.

While there are some exceptions, older persons tend not to be turned away from housing due to discriminatory perceptions about age. Rather the main barrier to housing experienced by older persons is a lack of housing to meet their needs both in terms of affordability and also in terms of accessibility.

It is the Commission's view that older persons benefit from the support, community, and income security offered by seniors' housing projects. As well, the concept of "aging in place" has been recognized by the Commission as a central consideration so that in some cases it may be appropriate to offer 'seniors' housing' to those under the age of 65 who may have special needs that will remain as they age.

Therefore, the Commission would encourage housing aimed at older persons, including those less than 65 years of age, which will foster the objectives of the Code. However, those responsible for such housing must be aware that age restrictions are prima facie discriminatory and that they must be able to justify them using one of the defences in the Code. Possible options include:

- Section 15: provides a defence to preferential treatment of persons 65 and over. This insulates housing that is limited to persons over age 64 from challenge by those too young to qualify.
- Section 14: permits special programs to alleviate hardship and disadvantage. This may allow social housing aimed at older low-income persons over a certain age, but starting at less than 65, if it can be shown that this group experiences particular disadvantage associated with their socio-economic status that younger persons do not experience. This might also permit specially designed barrier-free housing projects offered exclusively to older persons with disabilities.
- Section 18: religious, philanthropic, educational, fraternal or social institutions or organizations which primarily serve the interests of older persons, or older persons who belong to a particular religious or ethnic community, and which provide housing accommodation as part of their services may be able to restrict that accommodation to persons who are similarly identified. However, in order to rely on this defence, the provision of accommodation alone is not sufficient, some other "service or facility" must be provided.

Example: A synagogue runs a seniors' residence the purpose of which is to foster the religion and culture of its residents. Prayer services are provided and kosher food is served. It restricts membership to persons of the Jewish faith who are over the age of 60.

There is no defence, however, that will permit "adult lifestyle" housing that results in the exclusion of children or persons under a certain age.

Older persons may require accommodation in order to enjoy housing on an equal basis as other tenants. The person responsible for the housing, such as the landlord in the case of rental accommodation or the condominium corporation in the case of condominium units, has a duty to accommodate the needs and capabilities of older residents, subject to the undue hardship standard.

Example: A tenant in a rental unit develops arthritis and requests that doorknobs in her suite as well as to common areas such as the laundry room be changed from round knobs which are difficult to grip to handles that are suitable for persons with arthritis. The landlord willingly makes this change as it is not an undue hardship to do so. Moreover, it will benefit other tenants in the building who are also aging.

The duty to take steps to address special needs might include changes to an older person's apartment (except where owned by the person him or herself), building entrance, sidewalks, parking facilities and common areas. This might include physical modifications such as installing elevators, ramps, visual fire alarms and doorbells for the hearing impaired, different door handles, lower counters etc. It can also require other forms of accommodation such as waiving a rule, allowing transfer to another unit without penalty, providing better maintenance such as more frequent snow removal and so on.

Goods, Services and Facilities

Section 1 of the Code prohibits age discrimination in "services, goods and facilities". This includes but is not limited to educational institutions, hospitals and health services, community care access centres, long-term care facilities, insurance providers, public places like malls and parks, public transit, and stores and restaurants.

Older persons have a right to the same level and quality of services as everyone else and service providers have a legal responsibility to ensure accessibility, subject to the undue hardship standard.

Age discrimination in services can arise as a result of direct discrimination, for example through programs with age requirements that are discriminatory:

Example: An Ontario Ministry of Health assistive devices program provided closed circuit television magnifiers only to persons under age 25. A 71 year old who was refused the visual aid successfully challenged the age limitation on the basis that it was an under-inclusive special program. The Court noted that special programs should be designed so that restrictions within the program are rationally connected to the objective of the program. In this case the connection was not established, rather the program had age restrictions to have a small pool of clients and to conserve financial resources and not because younger persons had a greater need for such aids and less access to them.

Age discrimination in goods, services and facilities often results from a lack of access to services that meet the needs of older adults. As well, ageism persists as a problem with regard to provision of services and facilities to older persons. The social construction of age, which involves incorrect assumptions and stereotypes, results in perceptions that older persons are a drain on services such as healthcare and homecare or leads to undue attention being given to age when an issue, such as driving accidents, arises. At the same time, the other manifestation of ageism in services and facilities is the failure to take the real needs of older persons into account. For example, buildings may not be designed in a manner that promotes full accessibility, appropriate transit services may not exist that will allow older persons to participate in their communities and services may be structured around how quickly and 'efficiently' clients can be served with the result that insufficient time may be allotted for older clients.

The relationship between age and other Code grounds becomes particularly apparent when services are involved.

Example: A residential care facility does not allow a resident's same-sex partner the same visiting privileges as opposite-sex spouses.

Example: A transit provider offers a conventional service and a para transit system. Many older persons who have disabilities do not qualify for the para transit system and must struggle to use the conventional transit system. Therefore, the extent to which it is accessible (e.g. contains elevators, uses low floor buses, provides access to TTY phones and so forth) has a direct impact on older persons, particularly if they also have a disability.

Example: A hospital recognizes the need for food that is culturally appropriate for patients on its geriatric ward. It therefore makes arrangements for special meals to be brought in several times a week.

The right to be free from age discrimination in goods, services and facilities covers direct discrimination based on age and also policies, rules and requirements that appear neutral on their face but which have an adverse impact on older persons.

The three-step test to justify requirements that discriminate on the basis of age (described in section When are Standards, Factors, Requirements or Rules that Discriminate on the Basis of Age Justifiable? of this policy) also applies to complaints of discrimination with respect to goods, services and facilities.

As well, consistent with the Supreme Court of Canada's decision in Eldridge v. British Columbia (Attorney General), those who are responsible for the provision of services to the public must take positive steps to ensure that disadvantaged persons benefit equally from those services. Once again, this requires providing services in a manner that is inclusive and accessible from the start and also providing accommodation, subject to the undue hardship standard.

With respect to insurance services, section 22 of the Code provides that automobile, life, accident, sickness or disability insurance, group insurance or life annuity policies that are outside of the employment context may make distinctions based on age and other grounds but these must be made on reasonable and bona fide grounds. In Bates v. Zurich, the

Supreme Court of Canada stated that a discriminatory practice in the insurance industry is "reasonable" if a) it is based on a sound and accepted insurance practice; and b) there is no practical alternative.

Harassment/Poisoned Environment

The Code prohibits harassment on the basis of age. Harassment means a course of vexatious comment or conduct that is known, or ought reasonably to be known to be unwelcome. The phrase "ought to have known" introduces an objective element to the test.

In addition, the Code prohibits creation of a poisoned environment. A poisoned environment is a form of discrimination and can arise from even a single incident. It may be created by the comments or actions of any person, regardless of his or her status. The comments or conduct do not have to be directed at a particular individual.

Ongoing jokes and comments or derogatory statements made about older persons in a workplace or service setting, may constitute harassment or create a "poisoned environment" for older persons by making them feel uncomfortable, threatened or unwelcome.

Example: A worker is referred to as the "old fart" and teased by his co-workers about his age and perceived health problems associated with aging. He walks away from any conversation in which this occurs and from time to time tells people that he doesn't find these comments funny. When he mentions it to his manager, he is told not to worry about it as "it is all in fun since everyone gets old eventually anyway".

Even though comments and conduct on the basis of age may be perceived by some to be less offensive than if based on other Code grounds, there may be situations where it has the same negative effect on the recipient. It is important to remember that for harassment to occur, behaviour must be known or ought reasonably to be known to be unwelcome, but that this determination will be made based on the perspective of "reasonable person" which includes the perspective of the person who is being harassed.

8

UN Commission on Human Rights 2002 Session (fifty-eighth)

Since the World Conference on Human Rights in 1993, and the subsequent international summits and conferences convened by the UN, the annual sessions of the Commission on Human Rights have been characterized by increasingly sharp differences between UN member/non-member states. These differences have made it more and more difficult for the Commission to fulfil its essential function to promote and protect human rights. That is not to suggest that the World Conference and other gatherings created the problems; they were always there in one form or another.

Rather, the international meetings seem to have brought into the open, and placed in high relief, how far apart states are and how profoundly politicized international discourse has become. The lines that now so clearly divide governments and make concerted and cooperative action so difficult are drawn on any number of bases – e.g. the level of economic and social development, large or small nations, religion, race, definitions of culture, international action/justice or local remedy, the nature and character of political and institutional arrangements, access for states to international finance and trade systems, the nature and source of conflict within and between nations.

The extent to which the annual sessions of the Commission have degenerated into an adversarial exercise, in which progress in the protection and promotion of human rights appear to have become a secondary interest, was starkly apparent at the 2001 session. In terms of politics and substance it may be most remembered for two developments. The first was the open expression of anger, by parties on both sides, in response to the deteriorating situation in the Middle East and, specifically, the defence of provocation put forward by both Palestinian and Israeli representatives to justify either the second intifada or the response of the Israeli government to it. The second was the assault waged by a number of states on the integrity of the Commission's special procedures and, in some instances, the ad hominem attacks levelled at individual mandate holders (e.g. the Special Rapporteur on torture). The first issue was not resolved to anyone's satisfaction. The Commission did not find a coherent way to address the violence – state or non-state – or agree on the proper (or best) way to exercise its authority in response to human rights violations and abuses. In terms of the second area of controversy, the Commission generally managed to keep the mandates of the special procedures intact. Both the tone and substance of the arguments, however, strongly suggested that the greatest wish of a significant number of governments is for the system to fail, to collapse into itself, and to replace it with a vaguely defined approach based on advice and consent, so-called technical cooperation.

A third element in the 2001 session was not new but certainly underscored a problem that the Commission had consistently failed to address over a number of years. The session highlighted the near impossibility of the Commission having the time needed to consider the ever-expanding list of issues before it and to complete its work in an atmosphere conducive to calm and deliberate reflection. It was evident, even to the casual observer, that the time and the human and financial resources of the Commission were mismanaged. It was only through the impromptu scheduling of numerous night meetings that the work was completed and all those wishing to speak were accorded the time to do so. It was also evident that the statements given by governments, specialized agencies, national institutions, non-governmental organizations (NGOs), visiting dignitaries and others were often unrelated either to each other or to the subject(s) of the agenda item(s) under which they were putatively given.

The challenges posed by these three elements, in combination with a number of others, not only carried over to the 2002 session but were, in many ways, even greater than they had been in 2001 or any other year. The session could be characterized as chaotic, improvised and disputatious despite the best efforts of the Bureau and a number of delegations to guide the Commission through its work in a considered way. The reasons for the incoherence of the session were both political and administrative.

The following observations deal with several areas where politics and/or administrative decisions affected the capacity of the Commission to take decisions in favour of the promotion and protection of human rights on behalf of all persons, irrespective of where they live in the world. These points are specifically raised because circumstances are now such that participants in the Commission's annual sessions – whether governmental or other – seemed to be faced with a choice: (a) either the will is found on the part of all concerned to re-imagine the Commission and thereby ensure that it will remain central to UN human rights protection and promotion efforts, or; (b) the narrow interests of various groups will prevail and drive the Commission further (and faster) to the point of irrelevancy in relation to the global cause of human rights.

Administration of the Commission and related matters

The approach of the Commission to the work generally follows the pattern of other multilateral meetings: there are statements and, then, there are resolutions and/or decisions. What there very clearly is not is actual debate of the issues. It has been painfully evident for some time, to anyone wishing to see, that "never [or rarely] the twain shall meet".

The disjunction between these two activities would, perhaps, matter less if the Commission were still a gathering of a relatively limited number of governments but that is not the case. When established in 1946, the Commission had 18 states members. Since then, membership has been periodically raised — to 21, then to 32, then to 43 and, finally, to 53. At the same time, the number of non-member governments, participating as observers with all the rights and privileges this implies, also increased as has the number of UN specialized agencies, intergovernmental bodies, and NGOs that participate in the annual sessions. There have also been "newcomers" — such as national institutions (e.g. human rights commissions) and the human rights treaty bodies.

The number of special procedures has also steadily risen and, therefore, the number of mandate holders who must report to the Commission each year on matters arising from their work. As noted above, with more states, groups and entities participating it became common practice for the Commission to sit in fully-serviced night meetings that had been authorized by its parent body, the Economic and Social Council (ECOSOC). The budget implications of the practice did not seem to be taken into account in any systematic way by either the Commission itself, ECOSOC or a budgetary oversight body at New York headquarters (e.g. Fifth Committee of the General Assembly).

The Commission was finally pulled up short in 2002 when, approximately one week into the session, a directive was issued from New York. Faced with significant budget overruns in conference servicing throughout the UN system, the Commission's extra meetings that ECOSOC had previously authorized were disallowed. (Information indicated that, with the exception of the General Assembly and the Security Council, the directive applied across the board within the UN system.)

The effect of this one directive was to throw the Commission into a state of disarray from which it never actually recovered, despite best efforts by the Chairperson, the Bureau and others to manage the changed circumstances. It should also be noted that the UN Secretary-General, Kofi Annan, has made it clear that the Commission will not be allowed to revert to numerous extra meetings and that future sessions will operate on a basis somewhere between the previous practice of unconstrained use of resources and the rigid framework enforced for the 2002 session. This one fact imposes on all participants, including NGOs, the obligation to re-think the manner in which the Commission works and the manner in which they join in it – both during sessions and inter-sessionally.

At the outset, it should be noted that there was a general understanding that the measures taken at the 2002 session did not establish any precedents. Having be compelled, however, in some ways, to limit the participation of, among others, NGOs and those appointed by the Commission to various country and thematic mandates, it cannot be assumed that at least some governments will not invoke precedent at future sessions to accomplish the same purpose. With this in mind, among the areas that need to be considered in terms of adapting the Commission's methods and procedures to reality are the following.

Statements

As an exceptional measure, the Bureau reduced the amount of time available for speakers – member and observer states (statements and rights of reply), UN entities, national institutions, special procedures, NGOs and others.

The measures had particularly harsh consequences for the special rapporteurs, experts, representatives and working groups that make up special procedures. In a number of cases they chose not to give abbreviated versions of the statements that had been prepared. This was particularly evident for those with mandates related to civil and political rights and violence against women. The decision to take joint action and protest the Commission's decision to limit their time underlined their position that the procedures were not precedent. Separately and together they stated that the time allowed was insufficient to cover the main elements in their annual reports and/or reports of missions that had been undertaken. As a result, the summary records of the 2002 session will not reflect any of the content in the main and mission reports of these mechanisms.

The limits imposed on speaking time also had a strong impact on NGOs and national institutions.

In terms of NGOs, during consideration of item 9 (country situations) the Commission summarily declared an end to the "debate", abandoning some 30 or more NGOs that had not yet spoken. The compensatory decision was to issue the texts of NGO oral statements that had not been given as official documents of the session. As well, the decision to cluster agenda items towards the end of the session, coupled with a further reduction of speaking time, left a number of NGOs with less than two minutes to bring to the attention of the Commission their concerns and recommendations for remedial actions on either country or thematically based situations.

In terms of national institutions, it may be recalled that at the 2001 session, the representatives of these bodies were given seven minutes each to speak. Very few of the interventions addressed areas of general or wide concern. Rather, almost without exception, they focussed on the means by which an institution had been established, the mandate and authority it had been given, and the work that had been undertaken or was planned. As such, these interventions contributed little, if anything, directly to the work of the Commission.

With that in mind, the decision of the Bureau at the 2002 session to limit national institutions to one hour of time (leaving it to them to decide among themselves how to use that time) had virtually no effect on the Commission's work. The main effect was to minimize the exercise in self-promotion in which these institutions had engaged in previous years. In light of the fact that national institutions will not be accorded the same time as was given prior to 2002, and the lack of relevance of the types of statements that have been generally given:

It is recommended that during their private, coordinating meeting, the representatives of these institutions consider the feasibility of developing three or four joint statements to be delivered to the Commission on concerns such institutions may be reasonably expected to have in common (e.g. impunity, discrimination in housing and employment, violence against women and the failure of the state to exercise due diligence).

Since the statements of visiting dignitaries, governments, NGOs, and governmentally organized non-governmental organizations (GONGOs), take up at least 75 per cent of the time available to the Commission the question primarily is: What is their purpose?

- The statements given by visiting dignitaries (e.g. ministers of justice, foreign affairs) more or less: (a) emphasize the internal difficulties the government is seeking to address and the measures taken to ensure the protection of human rights — statements in self-defence or justification; (b) provide rhetorical support to the concept of human rights and the principle that violations of these rights are a legitimate concern of the international community; (c) name countries in which violations are said to occur and where remedial action is required; (d) indicate areas in which the government is interested in terms of devising an international approach to respond to problems (e.g. early-warning).

- Those given by governments can be generally sorted into several categories: (a) to defend the indefensible and to blame others (and history) for the violations and problems in their countries; (b) to criticize other states and to bring pressure on them to reform; (c) to blame the "international community" for failures or discriminatory treatment of one kind or another; (d) to outline institutional and other measures which they claim prove their commitment to the promotion and protection of human rights; (d) to carry on a state-to-state dispute and to indulge in mutual recrimination and an exchange of accusations.

- NGO statements generally reflect one or more goals, including: (a) to place on public record evidence of human rights violations in specific countries and/or regions; (b) to alert the Commission and, through it, the international community, of an emerging pattern of violations which, if left unattended, may deteriorate into a pattern of gross and systematic violations; (c) to be able to report back to members and constituents that the organization took action, however marginally, at the UN; (d) to propose to the Commission areas for action – e.g. impunity, a convention on enforced disappearances; (e) to support and promote the work of the Commission's special procedures.

- The statements of GONGOs generally reflect one of two purposes: (a) to carry out by proxy state-to-state disputes (e.g. India/Pakistan); (b) to support and defend governments (e.g. Cuba, Tunisia, China).

With few exceptions, there is no correlation between the statements given by one or more of these four types of speakers and the core of the work of the Commission. If it is granted that the efforts of the special rapporteurs, representatives, working groups and experts – whether country-specific or thematically based – are central to the purpose of the Commission then the question must be why so little attention is actually given to the results of those efforts. Or, at least, why so little positive and supportive attention is given.

The time constraints under which the 2002 session was labouring, and the decision of many mandate holders not to cooperate in their further undoing, meant that the content of a number of reports was even more marginalized than in the past and the considered recommendations in each of them received even less attention.

When devising new methods and approaches for future sessions, in light of anticipated constraints, the questions must be: Is the Commission sincere when it establishes these mandates and are all participants prepared to deal with each of the reports that is produced in a deliberate, coherent and thoughtful manner? If the answer to these two questions is affirmative, then it is very clear that states and NGOs alike must re-think the purpose of their prepared statements and the very nature of their participation.

Absent an unscripted exchange between participants and those entrusted with the mandates that form the core of the Commission's work the slide into irrelevancy will only be accelerated and the international community – states and citizens – may soon arrive at a point where their contributions to the Commission can be, for all intents and purposes, phoned in.

With these points in mind, it is recommended that the Commission seriously consider a technical separation of its work into two components:

1. Consideration of the relevant reports – both country-specific and thematic – of all special rapporteurs, representatives, experts and working groups as well as consideration of all relevant reports produced by the High Commissioner for Human Rights and/or Secretary-General, in an unscripted exchange between mandate holders and Commission participants; preparation of and action on resolutions and decisions which reflect directly the content and recommendations of the reports prepared for the Commission.
2. Concurrent meetings in which visiting dignitaries, states, NGOs and others seeking to place statements on public record may do so, with speaking time allocated on a basis that is equitable and does not disadvantage NGOs.

Documentation

The preparation and timely distribution of documentation became an issue for the Commission in the early 1990s and remains so. Shortly after the World Conference on Human Rights, a number of states joined forces and succeeded in formally reinstating provisions in General Assembly resolution 52/208 under which a 32-page limit on the length of reports was set. It may be helpful to note that the estimated cost of preparing documentation, in the six UN languages, is US $1,000 per page. As such, the limitation on the length of reports makes financial sense but may work against the interests of the Commission if the subject to be covered cannot be reasonably accommodated or adequately addressed. It should also be noted that in extreme cases where the 32-page limit was not respected it became the practice not to translate the document into the six languages and, rather, to distribute it in the language of submission or writing. The most recent example of this practice is the 2001 report of the Special Rapporteur on torture which contained entries in Spanish, French and English. The preponderance of the report was produced, however, in English, meaning that for anyone unable to read and comprehend English most of the report was inaccessible.

It may also be recalled that the reports of the inter-sessional Working Group on rationalization and reform of the Commission's methods and approaches reaffirmed the rule that reports must be available at least six weeks prior to the opening of the session. As a result of this rule the deadline for submission of reports is 15 December in the year prior to the session (e.g. 15 December 2001 for the 2002 session). The effects of this timing are several:

- At times, the information in a mission report is out of date. This is the case when a mission to a country takes place either late in the year and the deadline cannot be met or is not waived. It is also the case when a mission takes place in first three months of the year, immediately prior to opening of the Commission's session. In these cases, a report is not issued until either the next session of the General Assembly (approximately one year after the mission took place, best case scenario) or the next session of the Commission (as much as 15 months after the mission took place).

- The information in a main report does not fully reflect the cases taken up by a mandate (e.g. on arbitrary detention, torture, human rights defenders), does not include current information on the status of the case, does not include the response of the government, if any, to the communication or urgent action.
- The handling of reports does not appear to follow a coherent pattern. There appears to be no system in place to identify and process reports on the basis of immediacy or the relevance of the subject to the agenda and needs of the Commission. Rather, they seem to be processed in the order in which they are received. As a consequence, a number of pro forma reports prepared under the auspices of the Secretary-General, for example, are available well in advance of the Commission since they are frequently submitted between September and November. These reports often reproduce, either in whole or in summary form, information provided by governments, UN agencies and bodies and NGOs in response to specific requests (e.g. views on unilateral coercive measures). They may also be short reports indicating that little or no information was received, or that for one reason or another the anticipated action was not possible, or that the government concerned had not responded. As such, these kinds of reports are not substantive and barely receive mention by the Commission let alone consideration. At the same time, because of delays, the critical reports of country and thematic mandates, as well as those by the High Commissioner on specific situations or issues may be delayed and may not actually be issued in their final form until the Commission is already under way.

It is clear that governments cannot have it both ways. Having invoked the 32-page limit and the deadline for submission, it makes no sense for those same governments now to complain that the reports are incomplete, unbalanced and out of date.

The practice initiated for the 2002 session of making reports available in advance form on-line through the OHCHR web site may have helped resolve some of the issues. What has yet to be addressed, and must be if a re-tooling of the Commission's approaches and methods is to make any sense, is the need to establish priorities and ensure that the most immediate are met.

In the absence of coherence in the methods by which documents are processed and distributed within the UN system, it will be extremely difficult to establish an approach in which there is regular consideration of the reports produced, in particular, by special procedures and an unscripted exchange of views to the benefit to mandate holders, governments and NGOs.

It is recommended that the Commission request that, in the processing, translation, and distribution of reports, a system be established and priorities be established. Particular and immediate attention should be given to those produced by special rapporteurs, representatives, experts and working groups of special procedures (main reports, country-specific mandates, mission reports by thematic mandates) as well as situation reports of immediate impact and interest by the High Commissioner and the Secretary-General (e.g. Colombia, the Occupied Territories).

Access to sessional documentation

The pressures under which the 2002 session was working underscored a problem that has been around for a number of years, namely the difficulty observers and, particularly NGOs, have in acquiring documents that are produced within the normal course of business. This has been particularly true in terms of the texts of Chairperson's statements as they are delivered or immediately thereafter (e.g. on Colombia, East

Timor) and amendments that are tabled during consideration of resolutions.

For those who follow proceedings during consideration of resolutions. Again, governments cannot have it both ways. They often complain that NGOs are uninformed or unaware of how the Commission works and of decisions that were previously taken. At the same time, making it almost impossible for NGOs to follow the amending process guarantees that interested organizations are not able easily to compare texts and to evaluate for themselves whether or not the changes made benefit or disadvantage the cause of human rights.

The updating of Commission procedures at the 2002 session, by the use of electronic voting, has seriously compounded the problem for a number of NGO representatives. The system may produce greater efficiencies in terms of time but for many the "projection screen" on which the results are shown is almost unreadable and the outcomes are often not displayed long enough for observers to make a manual record.

The likely response to these concerns is that: (a) Chairperson's statements are posted on-line in a timely manner and the full texts are part of the official report of the Commission; (b) the amended texts of resolutions are also posted on-line and the process of amending is accurately reflected in the Commission's sessional report; (c) the voting results are available on-line the same day as the vote occurred; (d) with the voting completed there is nothing further to discuss with individual governments so immediate and "user-friendly" access to outcomes is irrelevant. These responses presuppose that all those who are interested and engaged have regular and immediate access to on-line facilities, ignoring the fact that there remains a huge technology divide between and within countries. They also presuppose that the actual means and manner by which decisions are taken are not of immediate concern to observers and that there is neither the wish nor the need to discuss with a government its decision to vote one or another on a given proposition.

It is recommended that the Bureau of the Commission, and the Secretariat:

1. Review the handling of sessional documentation and implement an approach that will ensure equal access to all relevant papers for all participants at the time a statement is given, amendment proposed or an action taken;
2. Take measures to ensure that the outcome of electronic voting is displayed in a readable format and maintained on-screen for an adequate period of time, and that the print-outs of voting are systematically distributed to all observers.

Intergovernmental and multilateral bodies

For several years the ability of the Commission to act effectively has been eroded as a result of the emergence of a number of intergovernmental, multilateral bodies. The first to make its unhelpful presence felt was the European Union (EU). It has been closely followed by, for example, the Organization of the Islamic Conference (OIC), the so-called Like Minded Group (LMG — Bangladesh, Bhutan, china, Cuba, Egypt, India, Indonesia, Libya, Nepal, Pakistan, Philippines, Saudi Arabia, Sri Lanka, Sudan, Syria, Viet Nam), and the Non-Aligned Movement (NAM).

At the 2002 session, for the first time, there was an agreed statement delivered by the Association of South-East Asian Nations (ASEAN) in response to the resolution on Burma. At the same time, the African Group (as defined by the UN) has assumed a higher profile and there has been a clear joining of forces by developing countries. In a sense, while the Commission may have only 53 members it has become a "Commission of the whole", in which each state participates through one or more of these groupings and through which individual states are relieved of their obligation to make their positions clear and to act accordingly.

The effect on the Commission can only be characterized as negative.

The 2002 session was particularly marked by a bitterness in which the bloc represented by the EU was vigorously opposed by one or more of the other blocs of states. The ultimate effect of this can be illustrated in several decisions taken by the Commission.

- The Commission discontinued consideration of the situation in Chechnya. The EU was the lead on the resolution. What has to borne in mind is that many of those living in that area are Muslim. In the past, Muslim states and the OIC supported action by the Commission in an effort to hold Russia to account for its actions in the region. Information indicated that, at the 2002 session, the anger and resentment felt towards the EU caused the OIC states either to vote against the resolution or to abstain, in other words to act against their own peoples' interests.
- The Commission also discontinued the mandate related to Equatorial Guinea in a show of solidarity among African states.
- The mandate of the Special Rapporteur on Sudan, an initiative led by the EU, was nearly voted down and maintained by only one vote.
- The efforts of the EU to have the Commission adopt a resolution on the situation in Zimbabwe failed as a result of a motion to take no action that received the unanimous support of both African and developing countries.

- The mandate of the Special Representative on Iran, again an EU initiative, was discontinued by a two-vote margin.

In a similar vein, it should be noted that the OIC called for a separate vote on the inclusion of the phrase "sexual orientation" in the resolution on extrajudicial, summary or arbitrary executions. While the amendment to delete this reference was defeated, the action by Pakistan, speaking for the OIC, raises the question as the to legal personality of this group of states and its standing within the UN. A similar question can be posed in terms of the behaviour and activities of the LMG, the Non-Aligned Movement, ASEAN and, indeed, the EU.

The point is not that states should not work and act cooperatively. Rather, the issue is the extent to which these entities may supplant or overwhelm the very structure upon which it has been agreed the UN is built (five regional groups that enjoy equality of arms) and the capacity of states to develop and pursue their own foreign and domestic policy objectives either alone or with others. It should also be noted that, using the EU as an example, the imperative that a common position be established on each and every question means that once a group of states has come to an agreement among themselves there is very little opportunity to negotiate with that group for changes to text or modifications to positions. In too many instances, the first text is the last text.

It is recommended that NGOs request from the UN a clarification of the legal personality and rights and privileges of such coalitions of states so as to understand better the constraints these entities currently impose on the Commission and to devise effective approaches to offset their negative impact on the Commission's capacity to act as and when required.

An associated issue is the election of states to the Commission. The composition of the Commission at the 2002 was, perhaps, the worst it has been in years. It should be noted that, with the exception of Canada, the Western European and Other Group (WEOG) was entirely represented by members of the European Union. Among the Asian Group there were a number of states that have consistently shown a disinclination to embrace the UN system for the full protection and promotion of human rights (e.g. Bahrain, China, Saudi Arabia, Pakistan). The presence of Cuba and Venezuela among the Latin American and Caribbean Group posed problems as did the membership of such states as Algeria among the African Group and, arguably, Russia among the Eastern European Group. It should also be noted that only twice in the past twelve years has a permanent member of the Security Council not also been a member of the Commission (the U.K. in 1991 and the U.S. in 2002). This would suggest that the Security Council's five permanent members are more or less accorded permanent standing, a situation that has a particular impact on WEOG membership since three of permanent five belong to this grouping.

During the 2002 session, several NGOs addressed the question of "criteria" for Commission membership.

One proposal was that, at minimum, all members of the Commission must have ratified the International Covenant on Economic, Social and Cultural Rights and the International Covenant on Civil and Political Rights. Were this standard to be used, the following states would not have sat as members of the Commission in 2002: Bahrain, China, Cuba, Indonesia, Malaysia, Pakistan and Saudi Arabia. If the goal of setting this criterion would be to eliminate those states that are seen as obstructionist and as working against the cause of human rights, this threshold of ratification would not significantly alter the character of the Commission. A more effective criterion along this line would be to require ratification of the six main human rights instruments — the two Covenants as well as the

Conventions on the elimination of racial discrimination, the elimination of discrimination against women, the rights of the child and against torture.

A second proposal was that in order for a state to be eligible for election to the Commission the government would have to extend a standing invitation to all the Commission's mechanisms to conduct in-country missions. As a minimum, this requirement would probably catch more governments in its net but also lead to the elimination of most, if not all, states in such regions as Africa and Asia. As a practical matter, action is not likely to be taken on the proposal; it is important, however, because it does keep the question of states' cooperation with the Commission's mechanisms firmly on the agenda.

With the principle of "equality of opportunity" accorded to states (with the exception of Israel), it is unlikely that any proposal to establish criteria for membership will succeed. At the same time, however, it is important to find an effective response to several concepts that have crept into the Commission's work in recent years or, have been around for some time but appear to be enjoy newfound support.

In terms of the former, it may be noted that Pakistan raised the spectre of "vital national interests" as possible grounds for not agreeing to the temporary measures proposed by the Bureau to ensure that the Commission could complete its work in the time available. The measures proposed by the Bureau included suspending or waiving several rules of procedure mostly related to speaking time and prior notice of actions under consideration by one or several states (usually in the form of resolutions). It is difficult to imagine any national interest more vital than the full promotion and protection of human rights for all but it is a near certainty that Pakistan was not referring to that and, instead, reserving for itself a margin of manoeuver in which to take up, yet again, the question of the situation in the Occupied Territories, the violence in Gujarat, India, or a similar matter. It may be helpful to recall that it was also Pakistan which introduced into the text on defamation of religions, in 2000, the notion that the Commission would remain "seized of the matter". In both cases, the concepts belong more properly in the Security Council and their relevance to the mandate and competence of the Commission is only marginal at best.

In terms of the latter — long-standing views that seem to have gained ground in recent years — a number of governments referred to state sovereignty and their absolute right to manage internal affairs as they see fit. It will be recalled that the World Conference on Human Rights reaffirmed that "the promotion and protection of all human rights is a legitimate concern of the international community". That reaffirmation was severely tested with the failure of the Commission to maintain the mandates on Chechnya, Equatorial Guinea and Iran, as well as by the refusal of Israel to cooperate with the High Commissioner by authorizing an immediate mission to the Occupied Territories so that a firsthand report could be provided to the Commission prior to the conclusion of its session.

On the basis of the 2002 session, therefore, it is recommended that all concerned and, in particular, NGOs:

1. Focus on how to limit the influence of states that clearly seek to narrow the scope of action of the Commission, especially with regard to the right of the Commission to consider country situations in which there are serious and recurring violations of human rights and to take all appropriate action;
2. Develop an approach that will effectively counter the increasing tendency on the part of some governments to use rule 65(2) of the ECOSOC rules of procedure – a

motion to take no action – to prevent the Commission from taking action on either country-specific or thematic issues;

3. Affirm, sustain and adapt the understanding concerning consensus that was achieved at the 1999 session — during consideration of rationalization of the Commission's work: namely that "as soon as the broadest possible agreement is reached" on a particular issue "all participants will demonstrate a flexible and constructive approach in order to facilitate a consensual outcome".

Non-governmental organizations

In 1996, ECOSOC adopted resolution 1996/31 which has made it possible for more national and regional NGOs to apply for and to receive ECOSOC consultative status. At the same time, a number of NGOs have continued to extend accreditation to representatives of groups that are not included among the organizations with consultative status. The combined effect of the ECOSOC decision and NGO practice is that each year the number of NGOs delivering oral statements has increased while the time available to the Commission has not. Faced with this reality and associated problems, there are some NGO representatives who have begun to question the wisdom of expanded access in light of the difficulties that have been arisen. While this questioning may not be popular and may even been considered heretical, it is necessary if a way is to be found for the Commission to function with any semblance of order and rationality.

At the same time, there remains a strong commitment on the part of NGOs and some governments to ensuring that, whatever changes may be made concerning NGOs, their participation continues and their right to speak and to be heard during deliberations is not so eroded as to make the exercise any more meaningless than it now tends to be. As painful as it may be, however, the 2002 session underscored in absolute terms the need for NGOs to re-think their role and participation. If NGOs fail to do so, governments will not and decisions on the future of NGOs at the Commission will be made by them and them alone.

A starting point may be to consider the nature of participation itself. A useful metaphor may be that of elections. A citizen who meets certain criteria (e.g. age, residency) partly participates in public life through the exercise of the right to vote. That right does not mean, however, that a person may go to the polling station and, when handed the list of candidates for that electoral district, demand to vote for a candidate on the list for a district in another part of the country. Neither does it mean that the same person, having cast a vote at the designated station, may then visit all the other polling stations in the town and vote again.

In terms of the Commission and the NGO presence, the right to participate in the work does not mean that one may speak at any time, on any subject, however many times one wants. In this regard, two things should be borne in mind: (a) up to the early 1990s, it was generally understood that country situations would be addressed primarily — and in some ways even exclusively — under the agenda item reserved for that purpose (now item 9); (b) NGOs were expected, and in some ways required, to base statements under all other agenda items on thematic concerns (e.g. torture, arbitrary detention, the right to development) and to address the content in thematic reports and comment on the recommendations.

As things now stand, several observations can be made: (a) between 1996 and 2002, NGOs have managed to turn every agenda item into a "country item", at the expense of careful consideration of all the work carried out by thematic mandate holders; (b) too often, the statements that are delivered do not bear any relationship to the actual subject that is supposedly under discussion; (c) there are a number of NGOs that deliver statements under four or more agenda items on, usually, the same country situation; (d) the right to participate is often understood to be primarily exercised through the delivery of oral statements when, in fact, the statements themselves achieve very little and other avenues need to be considered to achieve greater effectiveness.

The focus of a number of NGOs on country situations is partly explained by the fact that in some countries the space in which these and other kinds of civil society organizations may operate is severely restricted. It is also true that on both a national and regional level, concerned governments refuse to meet with NGOs to discuss issues of concern, the nature and scope of violations and remedies for those situations. As such, the Commission is often seen as the one place to which individuals and groups can come to place on record their concerns and to request the assistance of the international community. These two points need to be borne in mind but three questions remain.

- What further action can governments take on a bilateral or limited plurilateral basis to open up more space for civil society to function and to thrive in countries where this currently is not the case?
- What further action can NGO colleagues in more privileged situations take to help concerned groups and individuals make representations to individual governments as and when required instead of depending on one or more five-minute statements, once a year, at the Commission on Human Rights?
- What additional actions can be taken by those same privileged NGO colleagues, in collaboration with the

Office of the High Commissioner for Human Rights, to help the disadvantaged groups make greater and more effective use of the Commission's special procedures and the work of the human rights treaty bodies?

The scope of this report does not allow for a detailed consideration of how NGO participation may be adjusted. The following recommendations, however, may help as discussions of reform of the Commission's methods proceed and decisions are made with regard to the 2003 session and beyond.

It is recommended:

1. NGOs take the initiative and seriously consider further limiting the number of agenda items under which any one NGO may speak from the current ceiling of six to two or, at most, three items;
2. NGOs also consider what kind of training about the UN system may be required, and could be provided, to improve the effectiveness of thematic interventions so that they are truly thematic in orientation and correspond directly to the reports prepared by relevant mechanisms;
3. Consideration be given to providing training that will enable more NGOs to make effective representations inter-sessionally to the Permanent Missions in Geneva and, most certainly, well before the annual session of the Commission actually begins (perhaps through short briefing papers, with the information set out in point form);
4. NGO representatives with more experience in, and greater access to, the UN system generally, and specifically the Commission, make a greater effort to facilitate meetings for colleagues with relevant government delegations, staff at the OHCHR and the Commission's special rapporteurs, representatives, experts and working groups;
5. NGOs continue efforts to formulate joint positions so as to

reduce the number of statements that are delivered on the same situation;

6. Consideration also be given to providing training on the functioning of the human rights treaty bodies, how NGOs may prepare and submit "shadow reports" and how they may make maximum use of the concluding observations and comments prepared by a treaty body following consideration of a state report;

7. Bona fide NGOs with ECOSOC consultative status work with interested governments to develop the means through which the growing phenomenon of GONGOs – masquerading as NGOs and supporting actions by violating governments — can be adequately addressed and the abuse of participatory rights by such entities be stopped.

As noted above, the main outcome of five-minute NGO statements, especially on country situations, is to place concerns on public record. They are one of the least effective ways, however, to move the Commission to action. In general, a decision by one state or group of states to seek, or not, to take action at the Commission depends on other factors, including: (a) the publication of a critical mass of information in the media throughout the year or during periods of evident crisis; (b) the publication of a similar mass of information in the reports of several of the thematic mechanisms; (c) submission of a critical mass of information directly to the High Commissioner for Human Rights; (d) regular NGO briefings and interventions to relevant ministries, government missions and/or members of the national legislative assembly (again, throughout the year).

The lack of effect of statements, as NGOs now prepare and present them, is something that must be considered by NGOs themselves. This is especially true in light of the clear, coordinated and concerted move made by a number of states at the 2002 that resulted in the discontinuation of the mandates on Iran and Equatorial Guinea, as well as the closure of consideration of the situation in Chechnya and the obstructing of action on Zimbabwe. It makes little sense for NGOs to continue to use the same methods and approaches as they have for, at least, the past 12 years when the pressures in the Commission are clearly moving in other directions: most notably away from country-specific mandates and with an emphasis on advisory services and technical cooperation. That is not to suggest that NGOs should not bring to the Commission's attention country situations. The High Commissioner herself made this point in her statement to the Commission at its closing:

> We need to bear in mind that we might have reached a stage where the very success in highlighting and mainstreaming human rights issues in a more effective way could be in danger of provoking a reaction. One could see this in the voting on country situations, where there has been, at this session, a preference for an approach excluding action if consensus was not possible. The core role of the Commission is protecting human rights through drawing attention to violations and abuses must be retained. But it is clear that in the future it needs to be matched by a much more significant commitment to provide resources for technical cooperation and advisory services to assist countries in building and strengthening their national capacity in the rule of law, the administration of justice, and adherence to human rights norms and standards. Criticism will then be perceived as constructive and forward-looking, not finger-pointing in a judgmental way.

The High Commissioner also posed a question. "How will the Commission on Rights, the central human rights body in the United Nations, continue to discharge this duty of protection?" If the trend is, indeed, to phase out country mandates, then the "protective" function will naturally fall to thematic mandates and the Commission's detailed consideration of the reports that are prepared (whether main or mission). NGOs may be rightly sceptical of the effectiveness of advisory services since governments have used the programme in the past to avoid greater scrutiny and criticism (e.g. Haiti during the latter part of the Duvalier regime and the murderous activities of the Ton-Ton Macoute). It is one thing to act with a healthy dose of scepticism thrown in. It is quite another, however, to operate outside reality.

With these points and the statement of the High Commissioner in mind, it is recommended:

1. NGOs pay more deliberate and continuing attention to the OHCHR programme of advisory services and, in particular, (a) the areas in which the concerned government has requested, and OHCHR is providing, assistance; (b) the measures taken by that government actually to implement the programme in strict conformity with the terms of the agreement signed with OHCHR;

2. NGOs consider, in country-specific statements under item 9 (and, possibly, item 19) adopting an approach in which the "kinds" of violations are noted and the required reform and remedies are set out in point form for possible action through the OHCHR programme of advisory services and technical cooperation.

The situation in Israel and the Occupied Territories consumed a disproportionate amount of the Commission's time and attention. At times, the session took on the character of a continuing referendum on this one issue, to the near exclusion of all other concerns. Through coordinated action, the OIC exerted significant pressure and influence on proceedings and the Commission returned to the subject in more than one "special discussion". Under various agenda items, a total of eight resolutions and decisions were adopted on this subject particularly as well other such other issues as Lebanese detainees in Israel, the situation in Syrian Golan and Israeli settlements. Whatever one may think of the policies and actions of the Israeli government, past and present, and suicide bombings, the key point to bear in mind is that a number of the governments that kept returning to this situation are the same ones that strongly oppose the Commission maintaining its practice of taking action on country-specific situations. Neither these or other governments can have it both ways. If, in fact, their goal is to phase out general agenda item 9 then they must also phase out the continuing items on Israel and Occupied Territories and discontinue the mandate of the Special Rapporteur that they themselves succeeded in establishing in 1993 "until the end of the Israeli occupation of those [Palestinian] territories" (viz. not subject to renewal on an annul basis).

While "positive developments" were few and far between there are several which should be noted:

- the creation of a mandate on the right to health;
- the decision to place consideration of the rights of persons with disabilities on an annual basis;
- the attention given to the ratifications that were needed so that the actual establishment of the International Criminal Court can go ahead;
- adoption (by recorded vote) of the draft optional protocol to the Convention against Torture;
- the decision to establish at the 2003 session an open-ended working group to consider "options regarding the elaboration of an optional protocol" to the International Covenant on Economic, Social and Cultural Rights;
- inclusion in the resolution on extrajudicial, summary or arbitrary execution of "sexual orientation" as one of the

causes for such executions to be carried out against individuals and reference to the obligation of governments to investigate such killings and to hold those responsible to account;

- the request to the inter-sessional working group that was established at the 2001, to begin work leading the elaboration of a legally binding convention on enforced or involuntary disappearances;
- the decision to authorize the Sub-Commission to hold a "social forum" for two days prior to its 2002 session.

With the exception of the mandates on Equatorial Guinea and Iran, the Commission renewed both country-specific and thematic mandates, held by independent experts, as required.

Particular note should be taken of the omnibus resolutions on racism which was not adopted by consensus. The mandate of the Special Rapporteur was renewed for a further three years. The difficulties that may be encountered as a result of the resolution lie elsewhere. Understandably the text focussed on the World Conference against racism and related intolerance and implementation of the Durban Declaration and Programme of Action. Those governments that had previously objected to certain elements in the outcome document, and distanced themselves from them, did not support a number of provisions in the resolution. These included the establishment of an intergovernmental working group to deal with implementation of the Durban outcome and the establishment of a working group made composed of five independent experts to "study the problems of racial discrimination faced by people of African descent living in the Diaspora". The objections to these measures were both substantive and financial. In terms of the latter, the estimated costs for conference servicing of the meetings of these two groups is US $677,100. The required funding is not available and can only be allocated by a decision of the General Assembly. It may also be noted that the resolution establishes "a voluntary fund to provide additional resources" for: (a) implementation of the Durban outcome; (b) the participation of people of African descent and others in the session of the Working Group on people of African descent; (c) the activities of the Committee on the Elimination of Racial Discrimination; (d) national, regional and international activities to counter racism and related acts; (e) the anti-racial discrimination activities of the Anti-Discrimination Unit that has been set up in the OHCHR. While the goals of such a trust fund may be laudable the simple fact is that the Commission has neither authority nor the competence to establish it. That remains the prerogative of the General Assembly and the Secretary-General.

The last word on the 2002 session is simply that change is inevitable since the Commission clearly can no longer maintain practices that have, for all intents and purposes, been superceded by events. It remains for NGOs and governments alike to decide what changes will be made, for whose benefit.

Net Censorship Bill

The On-line Services section of the NSW Classification (Publications, Films and Computer Games) Enforcement Amendment Bill 2001 is a profoundly flawed document.

The Bill burdens freedom of communication online far more than offline. It treats the many ordinary people who use the Internet to communicate, as well as commercial online publishers, far less justly and fairly under criminal law than is applicable to speech and distribution of information offline. It demonstrates a clear objective to apply more restrictive censorship law to material online than applies offline, notwithstanding that it is claimed in the Second Reading Speech (but the provisions of the Bill show otherwise) that the Bill "is based on the principle that any matter that is illegal or controlled offline should also be illegal or controlled online".

The Bill is not reasonably appropriate and adapted to serve a legitimate end. EFA recognises that, unquestionably, there is much material on the world-wide Internet that is unsuitable for children and that it is desirable to protect children from exposure to such material. However, this Bill will not achieve that end. It will make no difference whatsoever to the ease with which minors may inadvertently (or intentionally) access "matter unsuitable for minors" or "objectionable matter" on the global Internet. Nor will it protect adults from unintentionally (or otherwise) accessing material that some adults find offensive.

This Bill will not protect children, but it will destroy their future. It fails to recognise that children become adults (it aims to restrict information made available by Australian adults for Australian adults to that fit for children) and disadvantages Australian participation in the global economy.

The Bill appears to lack constitutional validity. The co-operative classification scheme is arguably constitutionally invalid and the Bill confers additional functions on a Commonwealth agency in a manner that may not survive scrutiny. It is also doubtful the Bill is capable of operating concurrently and consistently with the C'th Broadcasting Services Act.

EFA strongly recommends that the Bill be abandoned. More detailed information on the reasons for this recommendation are contained later in this document.

EFA observes that the Bill was passed by both houses of the NSW Parliament without the slightest indication of an appropriate level of parliamentary scrutiny. EFA shares the view of the NSW Standing Committee on Law and Justice as expressed in their October 2001 Report on A NSW Bill of Rights:

"The Committee concluded that Parliament has a responsibility to protect human rights. This responsibility is not always exercised effectively. The NSW Parliament has at times been responsible for...passing legislation which breaches human rights standards. Legislation is prepared within bureaucracies without any measurement against human rights standards, and then passes through Parliament again without any, or at most ad hoc, discussion of such standards."

EFA commends the NSW Government, and particularly the Attorney-General, for their willingness to ask the Standing Committee on Social Issues to inquire into the provisions of the Bill, notwithstanding that the Bill had already been passed by the Parliament. EFA also commends the Committee for its willingness to undertake an inquiry into the Bill.

EFA hopes that the outcome of the Committee's inquiry will be recognition by the Committee and subsequently the NSW Government and Parliament that this Bill is not reasonably appropriate and adapted to serve a legitimate end.

EFA fears, however, that the inquiry may serve no purpose other than to further demonstrate the danger to Internet users' rights and freedom from legislators who lack adequate knowledge and understanding of the communications medium (and associated technology) they seek to regulate.

In the event that the Committee, Government and Parliament fail to comprehend the overall flaws in the proposed legislation, at the very least, serious criminal justice issues must be addressed and resolved to minimise the extent to which ordinary people in NSW who use the Internet to communicate will be treated less fairly under criminal law than offline publishers.

The remainder of this document aims to explain the problems with the proposed legislation and in some areas recommends specific amendments intended to address the worst excesses of the Bill. EFA emphasises, however, that even if all recommendations herein were implemented, these would not result in legislation that is reasonably appropriate and adapted to serve a legitimate end.

Background to the Bill

The Online Services section of the Bill is substantially the same as draft model national legislation issued by several State and Territory Attorneys General for public comment in August 1999. At that time, EFA received a letter from the then NSW Attorney General inviting comments and responded raising a number of criminal justice and technological issues. Although the current Bill contains a few very minor improvements over the initial draft model, it appears that legislative drafters have not understood a number of other important matters raised.

Further, the draft model "national" legislation was prepared prior to the High Court decision in Queen v Hughes regarding co-operative schemes and it appears the potential ramifications of that decision have not been considered by the drafters of the Bill.

In late 2001, a Bill was tabled in South Australian Parliament that contains the same provisions as the Online Services section of the NSW Bill. The SA Bill was referred to a Select Committee, which was chaired by the SA Attorney General. The Committee recommended amendments in its report of 30 October 2001, and the SA Bill was amended accordingly. However, it should be noted that the amended SA Bill had not been passed by both Houses of the SA Parliament prior to the date of the next SA election being announced in January 2002.

The two flaws recognised by the SA Committee also exist in the NSW Bill, one of which EFA raised in its submission to the NSW, SA and other State/Territory Attorneys General on the draft model legislation in 1999. However, the SA Committee's report indicates they were not familiar with existing SA laws relative to offline publications nor technological matters. Hence the SA Bill amendments did not resolve other serious criminal justice issues.

NSW Government/Parliament has the opportunity reject unjust, unworkable and ineffective legislation, or at the least, introduce amended legislation that is less unjust and unfair.

The Bill covers a wide range of information, not only material involving sex or violence.

"Matter unsuitable for minors" as defined in the Bill (i.e. material that is or would be classified "R") includes textual information and discussions about aspects of adult life that are potentially disturbing to minors.

During the three years ended June 2000, over 50% of films were classified unsuitable for minors ("R") by the OFLC because they contained "adult themes", not because they contained sex, violence or coarse language.

According to the OFLC Classification Guidelines, "adult themes" include, for example,

"suicide, crime, corruption, marital problems, emotional trauma, drug and alcohol dependency, death and serious illness, racism, religious issues".

Unless information on these types of topics contains "little or no detail and [is] generally brief" (as necessary for an MA classification) such information is likely to be classified R and the Internet user/ content provider at risk of a maximum penalty under NSW criminal law of $5,500 (for individuals) or $11,000 (for corporations).

The legislation, which treats textual information as if it were an entertainment movie, will restrict provision by individuals and corporations in NSW (and possibly some resident elsewhere in Australia) of a broad range of socially valuable information on the Internet including:

- News and current affairs
- Medical and public health information
- Self-help/support discussion groups

- Discussion on social and political issues
- Art works
- Court judgments and transcripts
- etc.

EFA does not contend that the proposed legislation will criminalise online provision of all information involving "adult themes", but it will make it a criminal offence to provide detailed and/or non-brief information, including information that is not illegal in offline publications.

Moreover, the vague and subjective OFLC classification guidelines and associated uncertainty as to classification will chill online speech to a greater extent than probably intended by the legislature. Many content providers, which include persons merely discussing matters in online discussion groups, will err on the side of caution, rather than risk criminal prosecution.

Objectionable matter ("X" and "RC")

EFA submits that material classified "X" and that classified "RC" should not be treated in criminal law as if it were the same.

Although there appears to be a belief that material classified X under Australian law contains violence, this is not correct. Further since the draft model legislation was issued for public comment by the NSW Attorney General in 1999, the material allowed in the "X" classification has been further restricted to ban the depiction of various legal sexual activities between consenting adults.

The treatment of X classified material (i.e. non-violent sexually explicit material involving consenting adults) and RC classified material (which includes "depictions of child sexual abuse or any other exploitative or offensive depiction involving a person who is or who likes like a child under 16") as if they were equally offensive is an illogical and transparently emotive proposition. EFA has no argument with prosecuting the publication of material showing sexual abuse of children and this can already be done under existing law. In the event that NSW law enforcement authorities consider there is any enforcement difficulty in relation to such material made available on the Internet, this is a matter for law reform of an appropriately adapted nature. It is not necessary to criminalise online provision of a vast range of completely different material, as does the Bill.

Moreover, it is obvious to anyone who chooses to investigate that NSW law enforcement authorities are unable to prevent the ready availability and sale of X-classified videos from shops in NSW. Effectively enforcing the proposed online law will be even more difficult and further bring NSW law enforcement capabilities into disrepute.

Further, under the Internet censorship laws of Western Australia and the Northern Territory that have been in place since 1996, it is not illegal to make material classified X available to adults online. It seems unlikely that the A.C.T. will outlaw provision of X classified material to adults online.

EFA submits that the NSW Parliament would be better advised to regulate the provision of X material online rather than attempt to ban it. Further information is provided in Section 8.4 - Material Classified X. In relation to material classified RC, the application of guidelines designed for movies to textual and conversational material on the Internet is likely to result in criminal prosecutions in relation to material that would not be suitable in a movie, but may be harmless in context of provision of textual information on the Internet.

Types of Internet content covered

Text on Web pages and conversational material

Although the use of the term "film" has caused some people to believe that the Bill does not cover text, the Bill applies to both text and images (both static and moving). The relevant definitions in the Classification Act are:

" film includes a cinematograph film, a slide, video tape and video disc and any other form of recording from which a visual image, including a computer generated image, can be produced,..."

" computer generated image means an image (including an image in the form of text) produced by use of a computer on a computer monitor, television screen, liquid crystal display or similar medium from electronically recorded data."

It is thus claimed by legislative drafters that because an email message or a web page, that contains only text, produces a "visual image" on a computer monitor, it is therefore a 'film'. As a result, text in on a web page is classified as if it were an entertainment movie, that is, using the same rules/classification guidelines as those applied to cinema films and videos.

Email

There is a fairly commonly held, but mistaken, impression that all email is excluded from coverage by the Bill. This may arise from the statement in the Second Reading that:

> "[The Bill] is not intended to catch material that is not stored and not generally available on the Internet. Hence, it does not apply to email or to real-time Internet chat."

Although the Bill does not make it a criminal offence to send an email message containing "matter unsuitable for minors" to a minor, it does make it a criminal offence to send an email containing "matter unsuitable for minors" to adults in some circumstances. In this regard, Clause 45D(1) makes it a prima facie criminal offence to send an email message containing "matter unsuitable for minors" to an email discussion list that is archived on the Web, regardless of whether all subscribers to the mailing list are adults and access to the archive is subject to a restricted access system. Furthermore, it appears that sending such material by email to a discussion list that has only adult subscribers and that is not archived on the Web may also be an offence.

In order to understand how the above situation arises and the extent to which email is covered, it is necessary to refer to both the Bill and Commonwealth legislation.

The Bill contains the following definition:

"Internet content has the same meaning as it has in Schedule 5 to the Broadcasting Services Act 1992 of the Commonwealth. ... Internet content...is defined so as...not to include ordinary electronic mail".

Hence whether a particular email message is covered depends on whether it is "ordinary electronic mail" which is not defined in the Bill. This term has been extracted from the Commonwealth Broadcasting Services Act 1992 ("the BSA)".

The BSA does not define "ordinary electronic mail" either, other than to state that it "does not include a posting to a newsgroup", although the word "newsgroup" is also not defined. Reference to the revised Explanatory Memorandum ("the EM") to the Broadcasting Services Amendment (Online Services) Bill 1999 provides an indication of the Commonwealth's intent. The EM states:

"The exclusion of 'ordinary electronic mail' from the definition of Internet content is intended to make it clear that the exclusion only applies to what an ordinary user of the Internet would regard as being e- mail, and that the exclusion does not apply to other forms of postings of material, such as postings to newsgroups. The term is also intended to minimise the scope for technical arguments about the 'outer boundaries' of the term 'e-mail' within the Internet community. The definition of 'ordinary electronic mail' makes it clear that the term will not include a posting to a newsgroup. These provisions are intended to ensure that personal e-mail is not caught by the definition of 'Internet content'.

Examples of Internet content include pages on the World Wide Web, archived mailing list messages, material available for general access from usenet news groups and information available from databases."

It appears highly doubtful that Commonwealth legislative drafters understand what "ordinary" Internet users "regard as being email".

Most, probably all, Internet users who send an email message to a group of people on a discussion mailing list regard such messages as being email. However, it appears the Commonwealth considers email is only email if it is "personal" email. Unless the NSW legislature amends the Bill to clearly define "ordinary electronic mail", it appears it will be a matter for the courts to determine whether an email message sent to a group of people is "personal" and hence whether it is exempt or not.

Nevertheless, it is clear that email sent to a Web-based discussion list or chat board, and email sent and received by email to a mailing list that is archived on the Web, is covered by the proposed legislation.

It is disturbing that the Bill places participants in email discussion lists at risk of criminal proceedings for events beyond their control. On some email lists, rogue subscribers have created an archive of email messages to the list on the Web without the permission or knowledge of the administrator of the list, nor of other participants in the discussion group. Postings to email discussion groups can also be gatewayed/ distributed automatically to newsgroups without the permission or knowledge of the email group's administrator or other participants. For example, this occurred with the Oz-ISP email discussion list in January 1998 when it was discovered by a participant that all postings to the email group were being gatewayed to a newsgroup and also subsequently archived on the Web by the DejaNews service.

Conversations in newsgroups

The specific exclusion of "newsgroups" from "ordinary electronic email" leaves no doubt that postings to "newsgroups" are covered by the Bill.

While the term "newsgroup" is not defined in the Bill or the BSA, it seems this would include, at the least, postings to Usenet newsgroups whether or not the particular newsgroup is archived on the Web.

However, as Usenet is a world wide network posted to by persons all over the world, the Bill will not have the slightest affect on the availability of material unsuitable for minors in Usenet newsgroups. In this regard, it should be noted that "matter unsuitable for minors" as defined in the Bill is protected speech in the USA. Further, neither the UK nor Canada have made it a criminal offence to post such material to newsgroups (EFA is not aware of any Western democracy that has).

Conversations in chat rooms and on chat and bulletin boards

Although it has been stated and/or implied from time to time that discussions in online "chat" facilities are exempt, only a narrow range of "chat" facilities are exempt.

Some types of chat facilities are exempt because the definition of "Internet content" does not cover material that is not kept on a data storage device accessible using the Internet. Hence "real-time" chat, such as Internet Relay Chat (IRC) and voice over Internet services are exempt (although not if archived logs/recordings of the chat sessions are accessible using the Internet).

However, other "chat" facilities such as Web-hosted chat rooms, chat boards and bulletin boards are not exempt.

Summary of restriction on online discussion between adults

The Bill criminalises the on-line equivalents of conversations among adults at a private or public meeting, in a pub, on a street corner, or at the local shopping centre when such conversation includes "matter unsuitable for minors". Posting material unsuitable for minors to a newsgroup, or any chat/discussion forum that is stored on the Web (e.g. email discussion lists that are archived) is a criminal offence under the Bill, whether or not the material is made available to minors.

The Bill will not, however, have any effect on the availability of conversational material that is unsuitable for minors through third-party off-shore ftp and web-based archives of discussion groups, use of off-shore web-based chat rooms and chat boards, etc. Furthermore, the Bill does not make it a criminal offence to intentionally and knowingly send "objectionable matter" to a minor by email.

As drafted, the intent of the Bill is clearly to criminalise conversations among adults involving matter unsuitable for minors, not to protect minors from matter unsuitable for them. If this is not the intent of the NSW legislature, significant amendments to the Bill are necessary. EFA submits that the application of guidelines designed for movies to conversations on Australian hosted chat/discussion facilities is a pointless restriction on freedom of speech and should be deleted from the Bill.

Comparison with 1999 draft model prepared for inclusion in NSW Act

The draft model national legislation issued by the NSW Attorney-General, and other State/Territory A-Gs, for public comment in August 1999, was less restrictive of adult conversations online.

The draft model stated that it was "in the form of a Part suitable for inclusion in the Classification (Publications, Films and Computer Games) Enforcement Act 1995 (NSW)" and included the following:

2 (2) Nothing in this Part makes it an offence to supply objectionable matter or matter unsuitable for minors by means of an on-line service:

(a) to any person in the form of ordinary electronic mail (within the meaning of the Broadcasting Services Act 1992 of the Commonwealth), or

(b) to subscribers of, or participants in, a chat or discussion group, or

(c) to any other person, or class of persons, prescribed in the regulations.

The above clause is not included in the Bill. It has apparently been deleted either by decision of the NSW Government, or decision of the Standing Committee of Censorship Ministers.

EFA submits that a substantially similar provision should be incorporated in the proposed NSW law. However, the exemption in the above provision for "ordinary electronic mail (within the meaning of the Broadcasting Services Act 1992 of the Commonwealth)" does not include email messages sent to discussion lists and postings to newsgroups. The provision should be amended to ensure that all email and newsgroup postings are also exempt.

Criminal justice issues and inconsistency with NSW offline laws

Material legal offline to be illegal online

EFA submits that what is legal to make available to adults offline should be legal to make available to adults online. Moreover, we note that the Second Reading Speech states that "The bill is based on the principle that any matter that is illegal or controlled offline should also be illegal or controlled online". However, in a number of instances this principle has not been implemented in the Bill, as detailed below.

Criminal offence to provide "R" material to adults online

Clause 45D(1) states:

"A person must not, by means of an on-line service, make available, or supply, to another person, any matter unsuitable for minors..."

This clause makes it a prima facie criminal offence to make material available to adults if it is unsuitable for minors, that is, whether or not access to the content is subject to an approved restricted access system and whether or not such material is provided to a minor.

This is contrary to NSW law applicable to offline material under which it is not an offence to make R-classified material available to adults.

While the Bill provides a defence, this places online publishers, unlike offline publishers, in a situation that is tantamount to guilty until proven innocent. In addition, there are criminal justice issues arising from the phrasing of the defence.

Furthermore, Clause 45D(1) seeks to restrict adults' communications more than laws applicable to online content in Victoria, Western Australia and thc North Territory. These jurisdictions' laws do not make it an offence to make R classified material available to another adult, as distinct from making it available to a minor. In conjunction with other aspects of the Bill, this results in cross-jurisdictional issues and uncertainty relative to enforcement of the law.

Clause 45D(1) also unduly exceeds the claimed intent of complementing Commonwealth legislation under which it is not an offence to make available material that is subject to a restricted access system.

For reasons detailed later herein, EFA considers legislation criminalising or otherwise regulating the making available of "matter unsuitable for minors" online is unreasonable, unworkable and will have no effect whatsoever on the ease with which minors can be, accidentally or otherwise, exposed to such material on the world wide Internet. However, if NSW lawmakers are determined to criminalise provision of this material, the offence should be limited to provision of material to a minor.

Criminal offence to provide "Category 2" Publications to adults online

Clause 45C states:

> A person must not, by means of an on-line service, make available, or supply, to another person, objectionable matter...

This clause makes it a prima facie criminal offence to make material available to adults that is legal to sell to adults in shops in NSW, without even providing a defence that access to the material was subject to a restricted access system.

This situation arises because classification guidelines developed for the combination of moving images and sound (movies) are applied to text and static images (publications) on the Internet. Much of the text and images legal in Category 2 Restricted publications would be classified X (non-violent sexually explicit material) under film guidelines and hence be illegal to make available to adults online under the NSW proposed law.

Criminal offence to provide advertisements suitable for minors

The Bill makes it a criminal offence to make available online advertisements that do not contain any material unsuitable for minors and that are not illegal to screen on free to air television.

The definition of "matter unsuitable for minors" in the Bill states:

> "matter unsuitable for minors" means Internet content consisting of...an advertisement for [a film that is, or would be, classified R] consisting of or containing an extract or sample from the film comprising moving images"

Hence, it will be a criminal offence to make available an advertisement for an R classified film that includes moving images even if the advertisement contains no material unsuitable for minors. However, an advertisement that comprises static images from the film would not be an illegal advertisement even if the non-moving images were unsuitable for minors (although it appears that the web page containing such images could be deemed to be matter unsuitable for minors and so illegal in any case). Apparently the purpose of the reference to advertisements is to prohibit advertisements that comprise moving images, including where the content of the advertisement is suitable for minors, but not to prohibit advertisements that contain text and static images. Hence, in determining whether an advertisement is illegal or not, the first issue to be considered is whether it contains moving images, not whether it contains material unsuitable for minors.

Films classified R are advertised off-line on free-to-air television. They are also broadcast on free-to-air television after cuts to comply with broadcasting law. Television broadcasters are not required to put in place "restricted access systems" preventing minors from viewing an advertisement, nor a modified version of the film. Yet Village Roadshow and Hoyts, for example, will commit an offence in making available on their Web site exactly the same advertisement that can be legally broadcast on television. Television broadcasters will be in breach of the law if they place an advertisement on their web site for a film that they are able to broadcast on television. Obviously, this legislation will criminalise on-line provision of material that is not illegal to make available to minors or adults off-line.

Further item (c) of the "objectionable matter" definition enables prosecution to commence in relation to an advertisement, not only prior to the advertisement being classified, but also in situations where it advertises material that has also not been classified but is alleged "would be" classified X or Refused Classification by the OFLC.

Attempts to criminalise advertisements on-line are very likely to result in a raft of undesirable and unintended consequences, ranging from well-intentioned content providers becoming victims of overzealous regulation to adversely affecting the development of the Australian on-line economy. The question of whether a web page hyperlink to another web page might constitute an advertisement also needs to be addressed.

EFA submits that the definition of either "Internet content" or "film" is adequate, there is no need to refer to advertisements specifically.

Criminal proceedings commence prior to classification, unlike offline

The Bill enables commencement of criminal proceedings against an Internet user prior to classification of content, i.e. in situations even where material is not subsequently classified "unsuitable for minors" or "objectionable". This situation arises because the offence provisions in the Bill refer to material that not only "is" but "would be" classified in a particular way.

This is contrary to NSW law applicable to offline material. Clause 59 of the existing NSW Classification Act

"Commencement of proceedings" states that prosecution proceedings for an offence under the Act are not to be commenced until "the film, publication or computer game has been classified". However, the Bill does not include an amendment to Clause 59 to cover Internet content, nor is a similar clause included in the Online Services section of the Bill.

Police are not specialists or even trained in interpretation of classification guidelines, nor should they be expected to be. The role of the police is to enforce the law, not guess what it is. While it may be argued that police would not commence proceedings against an Internet user unless they expected the OFLC to rule that particular content "would be" classified R, X or RC, no useful purpose is achieved by enabling the possibility of police commencing criminal prosecution on the basis of a wrong guess as to the classification.

There is no justifiable reason for treating online publishers less fairly under criminal law than offline publishers. EFA submits that it would be more logical to enable criminal proceedings to be commenced against an offline publisher prior to classification. In the off-line environment, movie/film, video and computer game distributors are required by law to obtain a classification from the OFLC because it is illegal to sell or exhibit an "unclassified film".

Penalties operate on a scale dependent on the subsequent classification decision of the OFLC Classification Board. There is, for example, a penalty for selling or exhibiting an unclassified film even if it is subsequently classified "G". Once a classification is granted, the distributor/ seller/ exhibitor has an absolute defence to criminal liability for distribution of the material, provided they comply with any restrictions on distribution relative to the classification.

In the off-line environment, it may therefore be considered reasonable to prosecute distributors in relation to sale, advertising, exhibition and distribution of material that "would be" given a particular classification.

They are required, by law, to obtain a classification and can thus reasonably be expected to know that they are engaged in a criminal act in distributing films, videos and computer games that have not been classified. However, the NSW law applicable to offline publishers clearly states that criminal proceedings may not be commenced until material has been classified.

In the online context there is no legislative intent to require persons who provide material free-of-charge on the Internet to firstly obtain an OFLC classification.

It is therefore unjust and unfair to enable commencement of criminal proceedings against online publishers prior to an OFLC classification decision evidencing that the material at issue was illegal to make available online. Doing so has the potential to traumatise ordinary Australians and their families who have committed no crime.

Criminal conviction enabled without classification of material

The Bill enables a content provider to be convicted for making available an advertisement without either the advertisement, or the material that is advertised, being classified by the OFLC. This situation arises as a result of the inadequate definition of "objectionable matter", that is:

objectionable matter means Internet content consisting of:

(a) a film that is classified X, or that would, if classified, be classified X; or

(b) a film or computer game that is classified RC or that would, if classified, be classified RC; or

(c) an advertisement for a film or computer game referred to in paragraph (a) or (b); or

(d) an advertisement that has been, or would be, refused approval under section 29(4) of the Commonwealth Act.

Item (c) above states that objectionable matter includes an advertisement for a film or computer game that would, if classified, be classified X or RC. However, the Bill does not require law enforcement authorities or a court to obtain a classification from the OFLC as to whether the material advertised actually would be classified X or RC.

EFA submits that the Bill should be amended to ensure that a conviction cannot occur on the basis of a mere allegation and/or guess that the material advertised "would be" given a particular classification by the OFLC.

Reversal of the onus of proof, unlike offline

Clause 45D(2) states:

> "it is a defence to a prosecution for the defendant to prove that access to the matter unsuitable for minors was subject to an approved restricted access system..."

This unjustifiably reverses the onus of proof. Instead of the prosecution being required to prove an offence has been committed, the content provider is required to prove their innocence. This is contrary to the provisions of the existing NSW Classification Act relative to distribution of material offline. For example, Clause 21(1) of the NSW Classification Act states:

> "A publication classified Category 2 restricted must not be:
> (a) displayed except in a restricted publications area".

In other words, the law applicable to offline distributors/sellers does not make it prima facie offence to display a Category 2 publication and then provide a defence that it was in a restricted publications area.

EFA submits that, like the law relative to offline material, the onus ought to be on the prosecution to prove that access to online material was not restricted, not on the defendant to prove the reverse.

Conviction enabled in circumstances beyond the control of the accused

The defence in Clause 45D(2) enables the conviction of an Internet content provider in circumstances beyond their control. For example, when the ISP/content host's web server equipment (that hosts the content provider's material) has suffered a security failure as a result of incompetence/mistake on the part of the ISP/ICH's staff or criminals breaking into their system and altering security configurations.

Furthermore, it is doubtful that a defendant could prove that access was subject to an approved restricted access system "at the time the matter was made available or supplied by the defendant". It is not clear whether "at the time" means at the time the material was initially made available on-line, or whether material is deemed to be "made available or supplied" at the time it is accessed by a person who subsequently notifies law enforcement authorities.

Moreover, there is no obvious means by which a content provider could prove a restricted access system was in place at any particular time in the past. What will constitute acceptable proof that a restricted access system was in place? Will content providers need to obtain, at the time they first make the material available, a sworn affidavit from their ICH/ISP, or from the ABA, or from a yet to be specified entity? Will they need to obtain a fresh affidavit each day, lest the ICH/ISP's access security system subsequently fails due to technical inefficiency or error on the part of the ICH/ISP, or as a result of criminals breaking into the ICH/ISP's system, or any other reason?

This provision makes ordinary people in NSW who make content available online at the risk of criminal penalties for events beyond their control. It is unjust to hold content providers liable for the technical operations of their ICH/ISP's servers and systems. Content providers who depend on their ICH/ISP to implement password security have no control whatsoever over whether their ICH/ISP maintains the security of such a restricted access system.

This criminal justice issue was acknowledged by the South Australian Select Committee and the SA Bill has been amended as recommended by the Committee (but had not been passed by the SA House of Assembly as at January 2002).

EFA considers the clause recommended by the SA Committee is a substantial improvement over the original clause. The amended SA clause is detailed in the recommendation below.

Conviction enabled without unanimous (jury) agreement on classification

Under the proposed law the OFLC Classification Board effectively becomes a jury for the purpose of criminal law although without "beyond reasonable doubt" criteria being applied to decisions, and without the need for unanimity. Their non-unanimous classification decisions are prima facie evidence of the classification for the purpose of criminal conviction. Neither a jury nor a judge is empowered to consider whether the material should have been given the classification the majority of the Board decided on.

While an appeal, i.e. an application for judicial review, can be made to the Federal Court, the Court is not empowered to assess the classification of the material. The Classification Review Board's opinion on a classification is final. The Court is solely empowered to decide whether the Board has acted in accordance with the law. As stated by Justice French, in his decision in the case of Michael Brown & Ors v Members of the Classification Review Board of the Office of Film and Literature [1998] 319 FCA (24 March 1998):

"The evaluation of a publication is a matter for the Board in the discharge of its duties under the Act. The function of this Court upon an application for judicial review is to decide whether the Board has acted in accordance with the law. It is not to substitute its own assessment of the publication for that of the Board"

Furthermore, in cases where content providers have placed unclassified material online, the Classification Board will be making a classification assessment in the knowledge that their decision makes the difference between whether or not a person will be charged with a criminal offence. This is not the case when they classify offline movies and videos because it is an offence to sell/exhibit any unclassified film or video offline.

The proposed law subjects ordinary people in NSW to criminal proceedings for failure to foresee the classification that "would be" granted to particular material by members of the Boards of the Office of Film and Literature Classification (OFLC). Decisions of the OFLC Classification Boards are not required to be unanimous and often are not. The OFLC Board members disagree over the boundary between MA and R material, as do many other members of the Australian community. In addition, the Classification Review Board from time to time disagrees with a classification granted by the Classification Board.

Given individual members of these Boards, trained in interpreting the Classification Acts, the National Classification Code and the Classification Guidelines are unable to agree on a classification, it is unjust to enable criminal proceedings against ordinary people for failure to correctly foresee the decision of the OFLC Board members.

Cost prohibitive to obtain classification pre-publication due to Commonwealth law

The Bill requires an Internet user, who wishes to be sure their content will not breach the law, to pay approximately $700 for classification of one page of text in electronic format, compared to $130 for a page to be published offline on paper. This situation arises because the Commonwealth has not prescribed classification fees specific to Internet content and the Federal Attorney General has stated that the OFLC will charge the same fees for a web page of text as for a cinema film or videotape. Further, in the case of a successful criminal prosecution, the court may order the online content provider to pay (reimburse police costs) an OFLC classification fee for a 'film' of some $700 in addition to the penalty. In the case of a web page consisting of three images and text, it appears the definition of 'film' would enable the OFLC to charge some $2,800, i.e. for four 'films'. This is unjust since the OFLC classification fee for an entire offline magazine is $130.

Offence Element: Recklessness

The usefulness of the "recklessness" element of the offence in ensuring a well-intentioned online publisher will not be convicted is highly doubtful because the matter of how any particular information would be classified is a matter of opinion, a value judgement, it is not a matter of fact.

The offence provisions (Clauses 45C and 45D) state:

"A person must not, by means of an on-line service, make available, or supply, to another person, [objectionable matter/or/any matter unsuitable for minors]:

(a) knowing that it is [objectionable matter/or/matter unsuitable for minors], or

(b) being reckless as to whether it is [objectionable matter/or/ matter unsuitable for minors]."

and "recklessness" is defined (Clause 45E) as follows:

"(1) A person is reckless as to whether matter is objectionable matter or matter unsuitable for minors:

(a) if the person is aware of a substantial risk that the matter is objectionable matter or matter unsuitable for minors, and

(b) that having regard to the circumstances known to the person, it is unjustifiable to take the risk.

(2) The question of whether taking a risk is unjustifiable is one of fact."

The recklessness element places content providers at risk of a criminal conviction if they make a genuine attempt to comply with the law and similarly at risk if they do not.

Content providers who make an effort to interpret the guidelines and assess the classification, but who make the wrong guess are likely to find themselves in court. The (in effect) defence they are offered is that they did not know, and were not aware of a substantial risk, that the matter was illegal to make available online. If they so claim, they can then be accused of being reckless as to risk. To prove they were not reckless they need to show, at least, that they tried to interpret and comply with the classification guidelines. In so doing, they admit they were aware of a substantial risk that their assessment of the classification could be wrong because the classification guidelines are vague, broad, subjective and the "correct" classification depends on a decision of members of the OFLC Classification Board, a decision which is not, under the law, required to be unanimous and frequently is not.

In order to understand the difficulties inherent in attempting to accurately assess the classification that would be given to material by the OFLC Classification Boards it is necessary, at the least, to carefully read and consider the following documents:

1. OFLC Guidelines for the Classification of Films and Video Tapes
2. Decisions of the OFLC Classification Review Board overruling decisions of the OFLC Classification Board
3. Community Assessment Panels Reports, prepared for the OFLC by Keys Young, 15 June 1998 and 2 June 2000

Persons intending to enact legislation that makes it a criminal offence to make available material online that "would be" given a particular classification by the OFLC and who have not made a serious attempt to gain a good understanding of the classification guidelines and process could be accused of both recklessness and wilful blindness. Those who have read the above or similar documents will be well aware that there is a risk that any detailed discussion of "adult themes" - which include "verbal references to and depictions associated with issues such as suicide, crime, corruption, marital problems, emotional trauma, drug and alcohol dependency, death and serious illness, racism, religious issues" - could possibly be classified unsuitable for minors, or perhaps even objectionable in some instances given the application of film guidelines to written text.

In the MA classification, treatment of adult themes is required to be "discreet". Discreet is defined as "with little or no detail and generally brief". Thus any discussion of adult themes that is not "with little or no detail and generally brief" carries a risk of being classified R, unsuitable for minors.

EFA considers that claims that research conducted by the OFLC shows that it is easy to know how material would be classified are insufficiently well-informed. For example, the Report of the South Australian Select Committee on the SA Classification Amendment Bill states:

"Experience with focus groups in the context of the Community Assessment Panels suggests that members of the public with minimal training can readily and correctly apply the film guidelines."

Firstly, it should be noted that only 1 of 18 films viewed by the panels was a film classified "R", and no films classified "X" or "RC" were viewed. This research thus provides no support for a contention that it is easy to know how R, X and RC material would be classified. Secondly, while panel members were trained, the hundreds of thousands of ordinary Australians who make material available on the Internet are not trained, nor is it likely that they ever will be. Thirdly, in many instances the initial classifications given to a film by panel members were changed after the group facilitator pointed out how particular aspects of the guidelines should be applied and/or other discussion among panel group members who had different opinions about the appropriate classification.

Moreover, an analysis of the first OFLC Community Assessment Panels Report (1998) reveals that of the total classification assessments made by the panel members, 51% of their classification decisions were not the same as the decisions made by the OFLC Classification Board. 29% of the classifications were lower than the Board's and 22% higher.

In the case of the Sydney panel members who assessed the only R classified film included in the OFLC research (One Eight Seven - psychological breakdown/suicide theme), 41% gave it an MA classification, that is, lower than the OFLC Board's R classification. If these NSW residents had been deciding whether or not to make content available on the Internet, on the basis of their assessments 7 of 17 of them would be guilty of an offence under proposed NSW legislation unless they could convince a court that they could not have foreseen there was a substantial risk the material would be rated R.

In a document issued by the SA Attorney-General in March 2001 (in response to questions regarding proposed SA legislation) it is stated that: "Adult themes are permitted in M and MA rated films. At MA level, for example, content such as in Saving Private Ryan (war theme) and The Green Mile (death penalty theme) and The General's Daughter (rape theme) can be accommodated."

However, both Saving Private Ryan and The General's Daughter were classified R by the national Classification Board and only became MA after costly appeal to the Classification Review Board. Further, 60% of a community panel who classified The General's Daughter while participating in OFLC research gave the film a lower classification (MA) than did the Classification Board (R).

Defence: Impracticability of approved restricted access system

There is considerable misunderstanding concerning the defence of an approved restricted access system, including apparently among some legislators. For example, the SA Select Committee's Report on the SA Bill states:

"As to arguments that this is invasive of privacy, the Committee considered that this was no more so than the requirement for age verification to enter an MA15+ or R film, or to enter licensed premises."

The above statement demonstrates complete lack of knowledge about the nature of the Internet.

In the vast majority of instances when adults enter a cinema or licensed premises, it is patently obvious to the staff of such premises that the person is an adult because they can see the person is older than 18 years. Hence, the person is not asked to provide identifying information proving their age. Online, content providers cannot see visitors to their site.

Legislation such as the NSW (and SA) proposed law requires content providers to collect credit card details, or copies of birth certificates or driver's licences irrespective of whether the person is obviously approximately 17 or 70 years old. Moreover, since it is not possible for the person to merely show, for example, a credit card or a drivers licence, they are required to provide their credit card number and details (including when there is no fee chargesd to access online information, as there generally is not), or a copy of a birth certificate or drivers licence, to the web site/content provider.

This is far more privacy invasive than merely briefly showing a driver's licence to staff of a cinema or licensed premises and involves serious risk of mis-use of credit card details and personal information from a driver's licence or a birth certificate.

Furthermore, the Bill provides no privacy protection for personal information provided by Internet users to web sites and the Commonwealth Privacy Act excludes content hosts and content providers whose turnover is under $3 million per year, which thus excludes the many content providers who are not businesses as well as small businesses online.

EFA considers legislators who enact laws requiring adults to provide credit card information or personally identifying information to access "matter unsuitable for minors" demonstrate complete lack of understanding and care concerning the security and privacy risks of using the Internet.

It should also be noted that the proposed legislation does not permit a person to provide people they know are adults (e.g. because they have met them) with a PIN/password to access to material unsuitable for children without collecting credit card details or a copy of a birth certificate or drivers licence. Hence a person who wishes to provide their adult friends with access to a restricted section of their web site is not permitted to do so without first collecting personal information.

Similarly organisations, businesses, academics, community groups etc are not permitted to make matter unsuitable for minors available to their members, employees, colleagues, etc without collecting personal information from them, even when they have met those people and know they are adults.

The SA Committee also stated:

> "The Committee noted that restricted access systems are available from a number of commercial suppliers on the internet."

The above statement indicates the SA Committee was not aware that the proposed SA legislation, like the NSW legislation, does not require the use of "a" restricted accessed system, but of an "approved" restricted access system, that is, a system approved by the Australian Broadcasting Authority.

Moreover, while the NSW and SA Bills give the State Minister power to approve a restricted access system, the BSA does not recognise systems approved by a State Minister, only those approved by the ABA. Hence content on the Internet can be ordered taken down under the BSA even if access to it is subject to a system approved by a State Minister.

In the two years since the Commonwealth Parliament passed the BSA, only one "restricted access system" has been approved under that Act.

The requirement to use an approved restricted access system is administratively onerous to the extent that few content hosts or providers would be prepared to incur the costs involved in their administration. The only system approved since 1999 is that of the Australian Broadcasting Authority ("ABA") and requires collection of credit card details or copies of birth certificates etc. The many non-commercial content providers (individuals, non-profit groups, etc) who provide information free of charge would have no cost-free means, if any, of checking the validity of credit card details or photocopies of birth certificates.

If the NSW Minister (or any other State/Territory Minister) intends to "approve" any other restricted access system relative to compliance with their jurisdiction's law, EFA submits that details of such intent and the particular system proposed to be approved should be made publicly available, and public comment sought and carefully considered, before legislation requiring use of same becomes law.

Moreover, the NSW Minister should ascertain from the Australian Broadcasting Authority whether the ABA would approve, under the BSA, the system proposed to be approved by the NSW Minister. If not, content could be ordered removed from the Internet under the BSA irrespective of access being restricted by a system approved by the NSW Minister.

Further information on restricted access systems is included in Section 10 below.

Enforceability issues

Definitions and Interpretation

"Classified"

Although the Bill is said to complement the BSA, the definition of "classified" in the Bill is different from that in the BSA. This may result in enforcement difficulties.

In the Bill, "classified" means "classified under the Commonwealth Act. Commonwealth Act means the Classification (Publications, Films and Computer Games) Act 1995 of the Commonwealth."

In the BSA, "classified" means "classified under this Schedule", i.e. under Schedule 5 of the BSA.

As stated in the Explanatory Memorandum to Schedule 5 (of the Broadcasting Services Amendment (Online Services) Act 1999) under the definition of "classified":

> "the classification scheme under is distinct from the classification scheme under the [C'th Classification Act]" (emphasis added).

The Commonwealth has not empowered Commonwealth officers of OFLC to classify "Internet content" under the C'th Classification Act. That Act does not mention "Internet content" and the Commonwealth has specifically legislated to empower the OFLC/Classification Boards to classify Internet content under a different Act, that is, Schedule 5 to the BSA.

Moreover, the Commonwealth Attorney-General has stated that the OFLC will not classify "Internet content" for online publishers, it will only classify material submitted to the OFLC in the form of a recording on a disk or on paper.

EFA submits the above situation is likely to result in prosecution difficulties under the NSW Bill, for example, concerning the use of an evidentiary certificate issued by the OFLC under the C'th Classification Act. Such a classification certificate would refer to a "film" while the prosecution would concern "Internet content".

The fundamental premise of the Bill, that all Internet content falls within the existing definition of "film" in the Classification Act, is a novel and untested proposition. Moreover, it may be problematic to prove that classified material on a disk is the same as that allegedly made available on the Internet. Issues in this regard have to some extent been addressed in the BSA, but not in the C'th or NSW Classification Acts.

It should be noted, however, that insertion in the Bill of another definition of "classified", referring to Internet content being classified under the BSA, is likely to result in other enforcement difficulties. The Commonwealth has not empowered the OFLC to classify content under the BSA for any entity other than the Australian Broadcasting Authority and a number of the provisions of the C'th Classification Act have no equivalent under the classification scheme established by the BSA.

"Internet content" and "consists of a film"

The Bill defines the term "Internet content" to have "the same meaning as it has in Schedule 5 to the Broadcasting Services

Act 1992 of the Commonwealth". However, the manner in which this term is used in offence provisions in the Bill differs from its use in the BSA and suggests enforcement difficulties.

In the Bill, offence provisions proscribe making available "matter unsuitable for minors" and "objectionable matter" which are defined to mean:

- "Internet content consisting of a film"

In the BSA, however, two different references are used:

- "Internet content that does not consist of a film or a computer game" (emphasis added), and
- "Internet content consisting of the contents of a film" (emphasis added)

In this regard, the Explanatory Memorandum (EM) to the BSA (under the definition of "film") states:

> "References [in the BSA] are generally to Internet content consisting of the contents of a film. This is because on the Internet material is usually not in the form of a physical object (such as a videotape) from which an image can be derived. Rather, what is of interest is the images and accompanying material themselves."

The EM also states that the BSA (in Clause 5) provides:

> "that for the purpose of...determining whether Internet content consists of the entire unmodified contents of a film, any technical differences between the Internet content and the film are to be disregarded. For example, if the contents of an existing film were transposed into a form which could be viewed on the Internet and that film had fewer pixels, or fewer frames, then it could still be taken to be the same film. If, however, 'scenes' in the film were modified or transposed, then it would no longer be 'unmodified'.".

However, the NSW Bill makes no such provision.

Furthermore, the Second Reading Speech to the BSA states:

> "provides for a classification procedure for Internet content that is separate to that applying to conventional media in the Classification (Publications, Films and Computer Games) Act 1995. This is on the basis that the Classification Act may not encompass all forms of Internet content."

It is clear the Commonwealth believed there may be enforcement difficulties if the BSA had purported all "Internet content" consists of a "film" as defined in C'th Classification Act. Nevertheless, this is exactly what is purported in the NSW Bill.

Film -vs- Publication: OFLC classifications for NSW police

EFA submits that NSW police practice to date indicates there may be some law enforcement difficulties relative to the definition of "film" being applied to Internet content such as text, data, static images, speech, music or other sounds.

Although the definition of "film" has not changed since 1996, and is not changed by the Bill, the OFLC has been classifying some Internet content for NSW police as a publication, not as a film.

Offence provisions in the Bill proscribe making available or supplying "objectionable matter" which is defined as "Internet content" consisting of a "film" which includes a "computer generated image" including an image in form of text. The definitions are:

(a) a film that is classified X, or that would, if classified, be classified X; or

(b) a film or computer game that is classified RC or that would, if classified, be classified RC; or ...

film includes a cinematograph film, a slide, video tape and video disc and any other form of recording from which a visual image, including a computer generated image, can be produced, but does not include:

(a) a computer game; or

(b) an advertisement for a publication, a film or a computer game; or

(c) a recording for business, accounting, professional, scientific or educational purposes unless it contains a visual image that would be likely to cause the recording to be classified MA, R, X or RC;

computer generated image means an image (including an image in the form of text) produced by use of a computer on a computer monitor, television screen, liquid crystal display or similar medium from electronically recorded data.

The above definitions have been in effect since 1996. However, in recent years, the OFLC has been classifying Internet photos and chat room discussions as publications, which are defined as "any written or pictorial matter" other than a film, computer, or advertisement for same. Apparently, either the OFLC or some law enforcement authorities are doubtful of successful prosecution on the basis of claiming that a static image or text is a "film" as defined by the Commonwealth Act.

Some examples of material classified as a publication by the OFLC for NSW police, according to the OFLC publicly available database, include:

- "F* a girl (said to be various child pornographic photos and stories downloaded from the internet)" - Publication (Computer Print-out) - 13 July 2001 (Applicant: NSW Police - Blacktown)
- "North Sydney Police - CBE Job 99/0059 (said to be free photos - child pornography from the internet)" - Publication (Comp.print) - 25 February 1999 (Applicant: NSW Police Service-City Central)
- "A4 size computer generated photographs of naked females" - Publication Comp.print - 27 July 1999 (Applicant: NSW Police Service-City Central)
- "Internet Chat-Room Conversation - CPEA (Untitled said to be)" - Publication (Photocopy) - 23 June 1998 (Applicant: NSW Police Service-City Central)
- "Eleven.jpg (Internet Photo)" - Publication (Unknown) - 31 January 1996 (Applicant: NSW Police Service-City Central)

The above examples show that some text and images from the Internet have been dealt with as publications, not films, in NSW.

It appears that a close analysis of the definition of "film", and/or the rules of acceptable evidence, may be necessary to identify why images on CD and computer disks have been classified as publications.

As the situation presently stands, if it is established that content providers can be successfully prosecuted for making available "films" that consist of text and static images, it appears there is no impediment to content providers also being prosecuted, regarding the same material, for offences relative to "publications". For example, a commercial content provider could be prosecuted for making available "matter unsuitable for minors" online and also for selling a submittable publication, since images from the Internet and computer disks have been classified as publications.

If a Web page or an image made available on the Internet meets the definition of a film under the existing Classification Act, then commercial sellers of information on the Internet can be prosecuted under existing law for the sale of unclassified films. Existing offences relative to sale of films are not limited to sale from shops, or by post, courier, etc. Further information in this regard is provided in the Section 9.2.

Two classification fees payable in law enforcement cases

Under the BSA, Internet content hosted in Australia is prohibited content if it has been classified RC or X (or R and without approved access restriction) under Schedule 5 of the BSA.

In instances where the Australian Broadcasting Authority receives a complaint under the BSA, and the content is subsequently classified (e.g.) RC by the OFLC under the BSA, the ABA is empowered to refer the content to State law enforcement authorities (LEAs) who may decide to prosecute the content provider. However, NSW LEAs will not be able to rely on the classification under the BSA, the content will need to be classified again under the NSW/C'th Classification Act.

As a result, unnecessary work will need to be undertaken by NSW law enforcement authorities, and the OFLC will be paid twice for classifying the same content (two times approx. $700 or more), once by the ABA and once by a NSW LEA. EFA submits this matter should be addressed and resolved in a way that will avoid waste of NSW LEAs' time and of NSW taxpayer/government funds.

Constitutional Validity

EFA draws to the Committee's attention that the Bill appears open to challenge on constitutional grounds. It is doubtful that the proposed law is capable of operating concurrently and consistently (in full or in part) with existing Commonwealth law, and it appears the State of NSW intends to confer powers on a Commonwealth agency in a way that may not survive scrutiny in relation to Commonwealth and State powers.

The Bill appears intended to form part of one, or two, "co-operative schemes" agreed between the Commonwealth and States/Territories. It is unclear from the provisions of the Bill whether it forms part of a co-operative scheme to regulate online content (i.e. complement the BSA) or the pre-existing co-operative scheme regulating offline content (i.e. complement the C'th Classification Act).

Under Commonwealth law, it is clear these two schemes are quite separate. However, the NSW Bill derives components of its provisions from both Commonwealth Acts. EFA submits that the end result of the interlinking of the separate schemes (as envisaged in the Bill) is a complex and unclear piece of legislation that arguably lacks constitutional validity.

Further, both the co-operative schemes referred to above were developed before the High Court decision in The Queen v Hughes [2000] HCA 22 (3 May 2000) (aka Corporations Law case) and the Bill is, in effect, identical to the draft model State/Territory legislation issued in 1999, also before the decision in Hughes.

EFA considers an observation of the High Court in Hughes to be pertinent:

> "60. Courts, including this Court, regularly speak in terms of the 'intention' of the legislature when interpreting

> particular legislation. This polite but unacceptable fiction has never been shown in starker relief than in the present case. So complex is the interlocking legislation, with fiction piled upon fiction, that it must be doubted whether any of those presenting and enacting it were truly aware of precisely what they were doing. It may be hoped that this and other recent decisions, together with the great national importance of the subject matter of the legislation, will encourage its early reconsideration and the adoption of a simpler constitutional foundation to reduce the perils that are otherwise bound to recur, possibly with serious results."

Information concerning the potential perils of the Bill is provided below.

Concurrent State and Commonwealth Law

It is claimed in the Second Reading Speech of the NSW Bill that:

> "Proposed part 5A inserts into the Act model online content regulation provisions devised at a national level to complement the 1999 amendments to the Commonwealth's Broadcasting Services Act 1992 dealing with online services."

However, the Bill establishes a separate regime that pays little regard to the provisions of the BSA.

The Bill relies on an underlying classification scheme that is specifically stated in the BSA to be distinct from the classification scheme applicable to "Internet content" under the BSA. It includes offences for making available content online that is not "prohibited content" under the BSA. In other instances, it seeks to regulate the same "Internet content" and, in some cases, essentially the same activity as is also regulated by the BSA. (It should be noted however that the NSW Bill may be enforceable against a smaller range of Internet content than the BSA

EFA submits that a range of discrepancies between the BSA and the NSW Bill, as well as undefined terms in both laws, are likely to result in contention, in the Courts, that the NSW Bill is incapable of operating concurrently and consistently with the BSA.

To the extent that the NSW Bill may be capable of operating (in part) concurrently with Commonwealth law, EFA considers it nevertheless invites challenge concerning the associated co-operative scheme/s as discussed below.

Validity of co-operative schemes - State powers conferred on Commonwealth

In EFA's view, the NSW Classification Act, including as proposed to be amended by the Bill, lacks constitutional validity insofar as NSW has exclusively conferred State powers and associated duties on a Commonwealth agency/officers in the absence of relevant Commonwealth powers.

This view is supported by steps taken in late 2001 by the Parliaments of Tasmania (Legislative Assembly 31 Oct 2001) and South Australia (House of Assembly 29 Nov 2001) to attempt to "Hughes-proof" amendments to their Classification Acts. (These amendments did not include provisions directed to regulating online content, and attempts directed to Hughes-proofing did not address portions of the Act that were not being amended by the Bills.)

As the Committee would be aware, the High Court decision in Hughes has brought the constitutional validity of co-operative schemes into doubt where:

- the State law requires action or involvement of a Commonwealth officer or agency to function
- the State law confers powers coupled with duties adversely to affect the rights of individuals
- the power conferred on the officer or the instrumentality to carry out the function is not supported by either the Australian Constitution or a law of the Commonwealth supported by an appropriate head of power.

EFA submits that all of the above apply to the existing "co-operative" classification scheme and may apply to a greater extent to the extension to the scheme concerning online content as envisaged in the Bill.

The scheme's application to offline and online content is addressed below.

Offline material

The NSW Classification Act confers various powers and functions on a Commonwealth agency and officers. In some instances powers and functions are exclusively conferred and in others the lack of a NSW agency or officer with similar powers suggests that the powers and functions have been exclusively conferred.

The NSW classification enforcement laws require action and involvement of a Commonwealth officer or agency to function and these confer powers coupled with duties adversely to affect the rights of individuals. For example, the Act confers exclusive power on a Commonwealth agency to decide whether material is legal or illegal to distribute, exhibit, etc under NSW criminal law. No NSW agency, officer or Court is empowered to make, or overturn, a classification decision of the Commonwealth agency. Obviously a decision to classify material X or RC (and to a lesser extent some other ratings) adversely affects the right of an individual, that they would otherwise have, to freedom of speech and to distribute, exhibit, etc the particular material at issue (whether the material comprises the individual's own speech or that of other individuals).

Further, the Commonwealth agency is required to certify the classification of material for evidentiary purposes in State criminal proceedings. No NSW agency or officer is empowered to do so. There are also other instances where the rights of individuals are adversely affected by powers and functions conferred by the State on the Commonwealth. The Commonwealth's powers to participate in this co-operative scheme in the manner conferred by the State is, at best, dubious.

While the Commonwealth has always played a role in censorship of material, for most of this century this has been through customs regulations concerning importation of various types of films and publications under the Commonwealth's trade and commerce power. This power does not, however, allow the Commonwealth to regulate the production and sale etc of material in the States.

The current co-operative classification scheme became effective on 1 January 1996, and the Second Reading Speech of the Commonwealth Classification Act states:

> "Reflecting the co-operative nature of Australia's censorship laws, the Bill is for a Federal Act for the Australian Capital Territory under section 122 of the Constitution. The Australian Capital Territory self-government legislation reserved to the Commonwealth the power to classify material for censorship purposes. This was to ensure that a national censorship scheme was preserved."

It seems clear that the Commonwealth considered its only (unquestionable) power to classify material for censorship purposes (other than in relation to importation of material) was derived from a decision to reserve those powers to the Commonwealth when granting the A.C.T. self-government. However, reserving this power to the Commonwealth in relation to the A.C.T. does not provide the Commonwealth with constitutional power to classify material for other jurisdictions. In this regard, the Second Reading speech of the Commonwealth Classification Act also states:

> "The Bill will only apply by its own force in respect of the Australian Capital Territory and the extent to which classification decisions under it have effect in other jurisdictions is a matter entirely for the State or Territory concerned ... the Bill, in order to preserve a national scheme, makes provision for the States and the Northern Territory to confer functions on the Classification Board under their own legislation in accordance with an agreement between the Commonwealth and the jurisdiction concerned. The Bill is essentially procedural in nature and reflects the current approach to censorship matters agreed by the Commonwealth, States and Territories."

As seems clear from various remarks in the Hughes decision (and prior High Court decisions), mere agreement by the Commonwealth, States and Territories does not necessarily result in constitutionally valid legislation.

While there are other Commonwealth heads of power that are arguably relevant to classification of material in specific instances, these are unlikely to cover classification of all locally produced material. Of course, if it is ever established that the Commonwealth has sufficient powers to participate in the co-operative classification scheme relative to all material, there would be a significantly reduced need for a co-operative regime. The Commonwealth could decide to exclude States from participation in formulation of classification/censorship law and to over-ride any such State laws.

Online material

Aspects outlined above concerning offline content also apply in relation to the proposed scheme concerning online content. Briefly, for example, the Act as amended by the Bill confers exclusive power on a Commonwealth agency to decide whether a Web page is legal or illegal to make available on the Internet under NSW criminal law.

It may be that the Commonwealth has appropriate power (under its "postal, telegraphic, telephonic, and other like services" power) to participate in a classification scheme relative to Internet content.

However, there is no indication that the Commonwealth has, or intends, to empower a Commonwealth agency/officers to undertake functions and duties conferred on them by a State in the way envisaged in the Bill. It is clear that the Commonwealth has empowered the OFLC/Classification Boards to classify "Internet content" under the classification scheme established by the BSA. However, the OFLC/Classification Boards are not empowered by the Commonwealth to classify "Internet content" under the C'th Classification Act as intended in the Bill.

While laws in Victoria, W.A. and N.T. have purported to regulate online content since 1996, the offence provisions are phrased quite differently from the NSW Bill. Further, it may be pertinent for the Committee to inquire into the number of cases concerning making matter classified R and X available online that have been successfully prosecuted under those laws and, if any, whether the accused plead guilty.

EFA considers the proposed online co-opcrative scheme may be a larger target for challenge on constitutional grounds than the pre-existing offline co-operative scheme.

The proposed online regime restricts individual rights to a greater extent than the offline regime (for example in making it a criminal offence to provide material unsuitable for minors to an adult). It aims to cover speech by ordinary individuals rather than commercial publishers, provides no reliable, quick and reasonably priced means for having proposed online content pre-classified and is more complex and vague than the offline scheme. The costs of challenging the constitutional validity of the law would not be insignificant for a defendant. However, given the broad range of speech the legislation seeks to restrict and the vast number of individuals and corporations likely to be affected if the law is enforced, funds and pro-bono assistance may be offered by a wide variety of sources.

Cross jurisdictional issues

Minimal prospect of uniform State/Territory laws

Although it is over two years since the Commonwealth Government introduced the BSA and said that all States/ Territories would introduce complementary uniform legislation, only two States have evidenced intent to do so. Further, the proposed NSW legislation is different in a number of ways from legislation that commenced in 1996 in Victoria, Western Australia and the Northern Territory.

With regard to the situation in other jurisdictions, in the latter part of 2001, the A.C.T. and Tasmania passed amendments to their Classification Acts relative to offline material (similar to the amendments in Schedule 1 of the NSW

Bill) but did not introduce Internet censorship laws. It appears Queensland has no present plans to introduce Internet censorship laws.

EFA submits that there is no greater prospect of uniform online content regulation legislation throughout Australia than there is of uniform defamation laws. In 1979, the Australian Law Reform Commission ("ALRC") recommended that uniform defamation laws applicable throughout Australia be enacted. Over 20 years later, uniformity is no closer, despite a number of attempts among jurisdictions to reach agreement.

In its Report the ALRC stated:

> "It is not reasonable to expect editors, producers and journalists to know and apply eight separate defamation laws in publishing newspapers and magazines circulating throughout Australia and in selecting material for transmission on national broadcasting and television programs."

EFA submits that it is even more unreasonable to expect the many ordinary people who make content available on the Internet to know and apply the online content regulation laws of eight jurisdictions. While large commercial publishers and television broadcasters have the financial means to employ lawyers to advise them, this is beyond the means of the many non-commercial content providers who make information available online free of charge. It is essential that jurisdictional issues, as detailed below, be resolved.

Jurisdiction in which offence occurs

The Bill invites constant enquiry as to the particular State or Territory laws at issue as the law does not specify in which jurisdiction an offence (making available or supply) takes place. It does not define "make available" nor state when or where content is "made available". For example, is content "made available":

- in the State where the content provider resides, or
- in the State where a user downloads the material, or
- in the State where the web server that hosts the material is physically located?

Internet content can simply and easily be made available by any content provider on a web server located in any State, Territory or country. It is as easy for a person resident in NSW to upload content to a host located in Western Australia or the USA, as it is to upload to a host server in NSW. Some Internet content hosts provide free web hosting facilities eliminating even the need to arrange payment for hosting services.

In practice, a content provider may not know where the server hosting the content is located, and may lack any means to find out.

Many ordinary users without detailed technical knowledge of the Internet who dial a local phone number to upload material to their "homepage" may assume the web server is located in the same jurisdiction as they are, yet the web server may be in another State, Territory or country.

As the proposed law is drafted, it appears the Parliament intends to leave it to the courts to resolve jurisdictional issues when the law is challenged in the courts.

The following scenarios demonstrate some of the jurisdictional issues relative to enforcing the law as drafted:

- A NSW company may have their company web site hosted physically in the A.C.T. If an employee or consultant resident in the A.C.T. uploads material to the company web site in the A.C.T. (that does not breach A.C.T. law, but does breach NSW law), who made the content available: the NSW company or the A.C.T. employee or consultant? Has the NSW company committed an offence under NSW law?

- A national company with its head office in Canberra and branches in other jurisdictions may have their company web site hosted physically in the A.C.T. Employees in various State branch offices may upload material to the company web site. If an employee residing in NSW uploads content to the web server in the A.C.T. (that is not illegal to make available under the laws of the A.C.T.), has the employee in NSW committed an offence under NSW law? Further, has the company with its head office in the A.C.T. committed an offence under NSW law?

- A Victorian-resident content provider may make content available on a web server located in Victoria, in a way that does not breach Victorian law, but does breach NSW law. (Under Victorian law, it is not illegal to make content available that would be classified R to another adult and the law does not prescribe use of an approved restricted access system). If the content on the Victorian server is downloaded by a person in NSW, where was the content "made available": in Victoria or in NSW? Has the person in Victoria committed an offence under NSW law?

- A content provider who resides in Western Australia may have their web site hosted by a national Internet Service Provider (e.g. such as Telstra Bigpond, Ozemail, Pacific, etc.). Some national ISPs have a variety of servers, that is, several hosting locations for Web pages. A content provider may not know where the server hosting their web site is located, and may lack any means to find out. If the national ISP's web server is located in NSW and the content provider in WA makes available material that is not illegal under WA law to make available to adults (e.g. non violent sexually explicit material/"X"), has the WA resident committed an offence under NSW law?

- A content provider resident in a State other than NSW may have their web site hosted by a local ISP on equipment located in their State. The ISP may be purchased by another ISP (e.g. national or NSW) who decides to shut down the purchased ISP's equipment and move the customers' web sites to web hosting equipment in NSW without telling the customers. If content on the moved web sites breached NSW law, has the content provider committed an offence under NSW law? Who made the content available: the content provider or the ISP who moved it? (For example, when Asiaonline purchased a Qld ISP, all web sites that were hosted on equipment in Qld were moved to hosting equipment in another Australian jurisdiction and customers were not notified).

EFA submits that the law as drafted appears intended to regulate the activities of persons other than NSW residents (as well as NSW residents). Hence, NSW residents will also be at risk of infringing the laws of other States/Territories that enact legislation of a similarly vague nature.

EFA questions whether there is any limitation on a content provider being charged with a separate offence in NSW and in every other State/Territory that enacts similar legislation.

Moreover, if NSW and other jurisdictions fail to clarify the jurisdictional aspects and one or more jurisdictions introduce more restrictive provisions than NSW, then NSW residents may commit crimes under the laws of other jurisdictions in relation to activities that are not illegal under NSW law. Introduction of legislation that does not clarify the jurisdictional aspects sets an undesirable precedent that is likely to have unintended consequences.

It is also important that jurisdictional aspects be resolved because the underlying classification schemes are not the same in all Australian jurisdictions.

The jurisdictions of Western Australia, South Australia, Tasmania and the Northern Territory have reserved the power to vary/override OFLC film classification decisions. Dependent on the jurisdiction, either the State/Territory Censorship Minister or Classification Board may override OFLC decisions.

Although the OFLC may classify a "film"/Web page and decide it does not warrant an R, X or RC classification, one of the jurisdictions listed above may override the OFLC classification and classify the Web page/film R, X or RC. This raises the potential for a content provider resident in State "A" (where the OFLC decision applies) to be guilty of an offence in State "B" (where the State Minister or Classification Board has overridden the OFLC decision).

A content provider resident in State "A" may have their content hosted by an ICH whose hosting equipment is physically located in State "B" and vice versa. Is the content "made available" to be subject to the laws/classification decisions of State "A" or State "B"?

Since serious criminal consequences flow, the absence of uniformity between State and Territory censorship regimes invites constant enquiry as to the particular State or Territory laws at issue and, inevitably, the imposition of a censorship regime based on the lowest common denominator - material that is legal to "make available" under the laws of every State/ Territory. The most censorious State or Territory would define what is safe to make available throughout Australia, and content providers would be required to know the idiosyncrasies of "community standards" and guess as to the possible decisions of Censorship Ministers or Boards in several States/ Territories.

EFA submits that either existing or proposed classification legislation must be amended to ensure content providers cannot be prosecuted for infringing laws/classification decisions of jurisdictions in which they are not resident. Unlike traditional media, where the place in which publication, broadcasting or distribution occurs can usually be clearly defined, the Internet by its very nature does not lend itself to geographical confinement.

Ordinary people in NSW cannot be reasonably expected to know the laws of every jurisdiction in the nation, and should not be placed at risk of criminal proceedings simply because they chat and/or publish material via an uncontrollable medium that crosses state and national boundaries.

Inconsistency with other Australian jurisdictions' laws

(a) State and Territory Legislation

Clause 45D(1) restricts adults' communications more than laws applicable to online content in Victoria, Western Australia and the North Territory. These jurisdictions' laws do not make it an offence to make R classified material available to another adult, as distinct from making it available to a minor. Further a number of defences other than an "approved restricted access system" are available, for example in WA and NT that "the defendant took all reasonable steps in the circumstances to avoid a contravention of the subsection".

Under the Internet censorship laws of Western Australia and the Northern Territory in place since 1996, it is not illegal to make material classified X (non-violent sexually explicit material) available to adults online. Further, it seems unlikely that the A.C.T. and N.T. will criminalise provision of X classified material to adults online, given this is not illegal offline in those Territories.

(b) Commonwealth legislation

Clause 45D(1) unduly exceeds the claimed intent of complementing Commonwealth legislation. The Broadcasting Services Act ("the BSA") states that Internet content hosted in Australia is Prohibited Content if:

> "(i) the Internet content has been classified R by the Classification Board; and
>
> (ii) access to the Internet content is not subject to a restricted access system".

That is, R-rated material that is "subject to a restricted access system" is not in contravention of Commonwealth law.

Furthermore, the Clause 45D(1) enables prosecution proceedings against a content provider to be commenced during a period when an ISP/ICH is specifically authorised by Commonwealth law to continue making the content the subject of the prosecution available to both minors and adults. ISP and ICH's are authorised by the BSA to continue to host and provide access to material that is likely to be rated R after the ABA becomes aware there is a substantial risk it would be rated R.

According to Senator Richard Alston's statements in the second reading speech of the BSA "Interim take-down notices have been limited to RC and X-rated content rather than R-rated content (without adult verification) because of the generally less serious nature of R-rated material."

EFA submits that content providers should not be subject to prosecution for provision of unclassified material which "would be" classified R given provision of this material is sanctioned by Commonwealth law because of its less serious nature.

Classification issues

Inadequacy of OFLC Classification Procedures

Classification of "Internet Content" nzot provided

EFA submits that the proposed law should not be implemented until the OFLC is able to reliably, and at reasonable cost, classify Internet content for persons who wish to be sure they would not infringe the law in making particular material available online. Further, the proposed law should not be implemented until the OFLC makes clear and concise information on its procedures and fees for classification of Internet content publicly available.

According to Answers to Questions on Notice in Senate, provided by the Federal Attorney General on 25 June 2001, the OFLC's procedures are inadequate and obtaining a classification certificate would not necessarily ensure that an online publisher could not be convicted in respect of the material classified.

The Federal Attorney General's answers included:

> ...The OFLC does not provide online publishers with a classification service that is specific to Internet content... (Q&A Item 4 & 5)
>
> The OFLC does not classify material on the Internet unless the content has been down-loaded or stored on a recording, such as on a computer disk, or printed out. (Q&A Item (7)(a))
>
> ... [Internet] content to be classified must be submitted to the Classification Board in a form that complies with the definitions set out in section 5 of the Classification Act,

> for example in the form of a recording on a disk, and must be accompanied by a valid application. (Q&A Item(6)(a))
>
> (4 & 5) ...Internet content in the form of a recording may be considered to be either a 'film' or a 'computer game' for the purpose of classification under the Classification Act. Accordingly, existing or proposed Internet content may be submitted for classification as a 'film' or a 'computer game' under section 14 or 17 of the Classification Act. Internet content that is submitted in a printed form, as a print-out, falls within the definition of 'publication' under the Classification Act, and is classified accordingly. ...

It is clear from the above that the Commonwealth Classification Act does not recognise "Internet content" (nor authorise the OFLC to classify "Internet content") and so the classification given to "Internet content" depends on whether the material is submitted to the OFLC on paper, or on a computer disk. In the former case, the publications guidelines will be applied, while in the latter case the film guidelines or the computer game guidelines will be applied.

However, classification as a publication would be of no assistance to online publishers as a defence to a prosecution because when the material is placed on the Internet it becomes an unclassified film, i.e. a computer generated image (including text), or a computer game and the offence provisions in the Bill refer to "films" and "computer games", not publications. The NSW Bill does not recognise that publications may be placed on the Internet, although legislation in the jurisdictions of WA, NT and VIC does.

Some material that is classified Category 1 and 2 Restricted (restricted to adults) under the publications guidelines would be classified X under the film guidelines, and some would be classified R. Therefore, obtaining a publications classification would not identify whether the material would classified R or X relative to offences under proposed NSW law. (However, under for example Victorian legislation, a publication classified Category 1 or 2 Restricted is legal to make available on the Internet, provided it is not published or transmitted, or made available for transmission, to a minor. Also, a number of defences are available in event of unintended receipt by a minor).

Moreover, the statement in the answers that "[Internet] content in the form of a recording may be considered to be either a 'film' or a 'computer game'" apparently refers to the OFLC Board's power under Section 15 of the Commonwealth Act ("Discretion of Board"). The OFLC is empowered to decline to deal with an application for classification as a film and may require the material to be resubmitted as a computer game depending on inter alia "the degree of interactivity involved". If the OFLC Board decides a web page is sufficiently "interactive" (perhaps because it contains links to other web pages) to require it to be dealt with as a computer game, material that would otherwise be rated R would be classified RC because the highest classification for a computer game is MA15+.

No procedure for classifying dynamic web sites

It should be noted that it is impossible to place some types of web sites on a portable disk for posting to the OFLC. The interactivity of some sites depends on technology of the web server (e.g. dynamic sites, database facilitated sites, etc), hence content submitted on a portable disk may have a different level of interactivity than when it is on the Internet. The OFLC Board is required to take interactivity into account when classifying and this affects whether the material is classified as a "film", an "interactive click-on access film", or a "computer game". Hence material on a portable disk may be given a different classification than would apply to content actually on the Internet.

Prior classification no guarantee against conviction

In instances where "Internet content" has been classified as a film or a computer game prior to it being made available online, the classification certificate may not be of any use as a defence to a prosecution. The online publisher may have to pay for a second classification and the content could be classified differently the second time. In this regard, we refer to the following question and answer in the Senate:

6 (d) what procedure does the OFLC have in place to enable them to identify whether the OFLC has issued a classification certificate applicable to particular Internet content, for example, where content is subsequently moved to a new address/hosting location on the Internet as a result of the publishers content host/ISP ceasing operations;

> 6 (d) ...The Board maintains detailed records of all classification decisions, including content descriptions and, in some cases, copies of the classified material for the purpose of future identification. In cases where there is doubt about the classification status of material submitted for classification, the Classification Board may interrogate relevant records to ascertain whether the material is identical to previously classified material. The Classification Act provides that if material that has been classified is subsequently modified, the material becomes unclassified. The onus as to whether previously classified material has been modified and therefore requires classification, lies with the applicant. Where there is

> enduring doubt about the classification status of material submitted for classification, the Classification Board may classify the material and issue a certificate.

The statement that the OFLC only maintains copies of classified material "in some cases" is of concern in the context of an answer to a question specifically about keeping copies of Internet content. It appears the OFLC does not intend to keep copies of Internet content that it has been paid to classify because, if the OFLC does, the question could easily have been answered accordingly.

Unless the OFLC keeps copies of classified content, a certificate will be of no use whatsoever to an Internet publisher alleged by police to have made available "objectionable matter" or "matter unsuitable for minors" because the OFLC will not have any way of knowing whether the content is identical to the content they classified. Therefore, there will be "enduring doubt" and the OFLC "may" classify it again (and charge a second fee for classification of the same material). In the interim, the members of the Classification Board and/or the classification guidelines, may well have changed resulting in the material being given a more restrictive classification the second time.

This situation makes it irrelevant that Net content is dynamic and often changed. Obtaining a classification certificate prior to making the material available online would not provide assurance against criminal conviction even if the content is never changed.

Exorbitant fees for classification

While it has been claimed that the OFLC does classify "Internet content", if it is copied onto a portable computer disk and submitted, both the OFLC and the Federal Attorney-General are apparently unable or unwilling to advise of the relevant classification fees. The following question and answer was tabled in the Senate:

> 6 (e) what is the amount of the fee charged to online publishers for classification of Internet content consisting of a web page containing solely of text and non-moving i m a g e s ;
> (f) is the classification fee referred to in (e) prescribed in the Schedule to the Commonwealth classification regulations; if so, is the fee based on running time of a film (minimum $770) or is the fee that is applicable to publications such as magazines and books ($130);
>
> 6 (e) and (f) The Classification (Publications, Films and Computer Games) Regulations (the Regulations), Schedule 1, set out the fees for classification. If the content is submitted for classification as a 'film' the fee will be calculated on the running time of the 'film' unless it is an 'interactive film', in which case the fees prescribed for 'interactive films' will apply. If the content comprises a 'computer game' and is submitted accordingly, the prescribed fees for 'computer games' will apply. If a print-out of the content is submitted for classification as a 'publication', the fee will be calculated in accordance with the prescribed fees for 'publications'.

The answer provides no guidance as to actual fees because fees depend on what the OFLC regards as a "film" and what type of "film". For example:

> If a web page contains text and 3 static images, when the material is placed on a portable disk and sent to the OFLC there would be 4 files on the disk, each of them fitting the definition of a "film". Will the applicant be charged for one film or four films? (i.e. approx. $700 or approx $2,800).

- Classification fees for "films" are based on "running time". For how long does a web site "run"?
- If the particular Internet content (web page/film) is not interactive, does the OFLC charge the fee for classification of a film for sale or hire (min. $510), or for a film for public exhibition (min. $770)?

Furthermore, it appears NSW residents outside Sydney would be unfairly discriminated against in instances of material the OFLC regards as an "interactive click-on access film" since the fee is $690 if the applicant demonstrates the material to the OFLC, which is located in Sydney, otherwise the fee is $1490 for non-demonstrated material.

It is also unjust to charge fees for films when the material at issue is, for example, one image or a web page of text, since the fee for classification of an entire offline magazine is $130.

Prescribed fees are:

- A film (0-15 minutes) for public exhibition: $770
- A film (0-15 minutes) for sale or hire: $510
- An interactive or click-on access film, if demonstrated by the applicant: $690
- An interactive or click-on access film, if not demonstrated by the applicant: $1490
- A computer game, if the application for classification is accompanied by an assessment of the game by an authorised person - $360
- A computer game other than a computer game specified above - $590

It is clear from these answers that no proper procedures had been put in place to classify Internet content and no other information on procedures and fees has since been announced or made publicly available. It is totally unacceptable for

Internet publishers to be faced with the level of confusion exhibited in the answers over whether Internet content should be classified as a film, as a publication, or as a computer game.

EFA submits that the classification system is quite clearly unable to cope with the particular characteristics of Internet content, namely any material submitted for classification can at best be an attempt to capture the content at a single point in time.

To suggest that a typical website with a mix of text, static images and hyperlinks is analogous to a movie film displays a breathtakingly superficial appreciation of the problem. The legislation clearly cannot proceed when such confusion exists about the basic premise on which it is based - namely that online content can be classified in the same way as traditional media.

The inability of the OFLC to cheaply and reliably classify web site content shows the NSW Parliament would be wrong to outsource its Internet censorship to the OFLC.

Application of movie/film classification guidelines to text

It should be noted that all on-line content is to be subject to classification under guidelines for films, even in cases where content consists entirely of written text.

The difficulties inherent in attempting to assess how the OFLC Classification Board would classify particular material will be exacerbated by the requirement that Internet content be classified using guidelines for films. Film guidelines were developed for entertainment material involving moving images and sound on the basis that such material has more impact on the viewer than written text and static images. Film guidelines are therefore more restrictive than guidelines for publications and applying them to Internet content is very likely to result in material that is legally available in publications off-line being illegal on-line.

In addition, film guidelines are written in a manner that makes their interpretation relative to written text and static images extremely difficult if not impossible. It appears this has been recognised by Censorship Ministers who agreed on 27 July 2000 to review the guidelines in view of concerns raised at the meeting that the film guidelines were less than adequate and perhaps unsuitable for assessing Internet content.

However, this review did not commence until 2001 and, based on previous reviews, it is unlikely that revised guidelines will be agreed and approved by the Censorship Ministers prior to the latter half of 2002.

Material Classified R ("Matter Unsuitable for Minors")

Material classified R is not limited to that involving explicit sex or violence. There is a broad range of socially valuable information likely to attract an R classification because it may be disturbing to minors.

In addition, the difficulties inherent in guessing what classification would be given to material by members of the OFLC Classification Boards, as discussed in Sections 6.1 and Section 6.8, has the potential to result in criminal prosecution of well-intentioned content providers. Moreover, uncertainty as to classification will chill online speech to a greater extent than intended by the Parliament. Many content providers will err on the side of caution, rather than risk criminal prosecution.

While the proposed legislation offers a defence of access being subject to an approved restricted access system, this defence not only reverses the onus of proof, but is impractical and unworkable in the context of the vast majority of material that is or would be classified R. The effect of requiring an approved restricted access system is, in effect, the same as banning the provision of R material online in NSW. As detailed in Section 10, most commonly used search engines do not index material protected by access controls, hence it will be difficult, if not impossible, to find Australian material, it will be easier to find readily accessible material on overseas sites.

Further, most Internet users will not bother going through a verification procedure. On the Web, attention spans are short and barriers to access are low. Even a minor extra barrier will deter people. A simple registration requirement has this effect and a requirement to submit credit card details or a birth certificate, as in the case of the only approved restricted access system, with all the privacy concerns that raises, will deter almost all visitors who will instead access overseas sites.

Commonwealth and proposed NSW legislation does not provide any control whatsoever on overseas sites providing material that is or would be classified R. The imposition of access control systems on Australian sites will therefore have no effect on the unrestricted availability of R-rated material to minors, since it only affects the 1 or 2% of content hosted in Australia. In order to protect children from material that would be classified R, there will be an ongoing need for parents and educators to supervise the access of those in their care.

Material Classified X ("Objectionable Matter")

EFA submits that material classified "X" and that classified "RC" should not be treated in criminal law as if it were the same.

EFA notes that it was stated in the answer to a question without notice in the NSW Legislative Assembly on 25 October, 2001, that:

"The amendments will make it illegal to make available or to supply objectionable matter to the Internet that would be refused classification or would be classified X for its explicit sexual or violent content."

However, material classified "X" under Australian law does not include violent content. Moreover, since the draft model legislation was issued for public comment by the NSW Attorney General in 1999, the material allowed in the "X" classification has been further restricted to ban the depiction of various legal sexual activities between consenting adults.

EFA considers the definition of "objectionable matter" should be amended to exclude material that is or would be classified "X". Such material would more appropriately be included in a separate category, titled "non-violent sexually explicit matter", that is not illegal to make available to adults who wish to view it on the Internet.

The application of guidelines developed for movies and videos to text and static images on the Internet will result in material equivalent to that in Category 2. Restricted publications being classified X (non-violent sexually explicit material) online.

In October 1997 during a speech at Murdoch University, Federal Attorney-General Darryl Williams explained the basis of Australia's censorship system, that is, the concept of classifying material on the basis of the views of reasonable adults. He said:

The 'reasonable adult' test is used in two different senses - as a measure of community standards and also as an acknowledgment that adults have different personal tastes.

The 'community standards' test, to be taken into account in making classification decisions, refers to 'the standards of morality, decency and propriety generally accepted by reasonable adults'. It is usually applied in the context of refusing classification to material.

One of the criteria for determining whether a film should be classified 'R' or 'X' or a publication given a restricted classification is whether the material is 'likely to cause offence to a reasonable adult'. This is the other sense in which the 'reasonable adult' test occurs and acknowledges that individuals may have different personal tastes. In other words, although some reasonable adults may find the material offensive, and thus justify a restricted classification for it, others may not. They should be allowed to have access to the material if they wish.

EFA submits that, at least in the on-line context, effect should be given by Commonwealth, State and Territory governments to the concept that "although some reasonable adults may find [non-violent sexually explicit] material offensive, and thus justify a restricted classification for it, others may not. They should be allowed to have access to the material if they wish."

EFA submits that the current bans on sale of X classified videos are misguided and result from misinformation.

In 1988, the Joint Select Committee on Video Material recommended "a new category NVE (non-violent erotica) be instituted" to precisely define the material contained within the X category. No evidence was found that viewing such material causes harm. Although implications to the contrary are promulgated by some people from time to time, the majority of the Joint Select Committee did not recommend a ban on all non-violent erotica.

It seems clear that bans in Australia reflect attempts to enforce the "community standards" desired by some people on other people, rather than reflecting community opinion or attempting to prevent harm. Surveys and opinion polls conducted since 1992 by the OFLC, the ABA and reputable public opinion research organisations have consistently shown that 70% (or more) of Australian adults believe that non-violent sexually explicit material should be available to adults who wish to view it. Australia is becoming one of the few English-speaking countries that continue to deny adults the freedom to publish and read sexually explicit material.

EFA calls on the NSW Government not to criminalise content providers who make available material that would be classified X. Many Australian adults wish to view such material and if Australian content providers are not permitted to make it available, Australians will simply pay overseas content providers for access to such material, as well as access it on free overseas sites. (The Commonwealth legislation (the BSA) has no effect on the availability of on-line material that would be classified X to Australians who wish to view it.) To encourage Australians to spend their money overseas is detrimental to Australia's economy, in addition to contravening Australia's international obligations as a signatory to the Universal Declaration of Human Rights and the International Covenant on Civil and Political Rights (ICCPR).

Material Refused Classification (RC)

Of significant concern in the area of RC material is the criminalisation of text thought to incite or instruct in matters of crime. In this area, access to the variety of material on the Internet may include access to material that would not be a suitable subject for a movie, but may be harmless in context.

For example, bans on teaching burglary techniques should not also ban a lockmaker's web site providing information to locksmiths.

In Australia, the OFLC's decision on the La Trobe University Student Journal Rabelais article, leading to prosecution for publication of Refused Classification material, is a dangerous precedent for the OFLC's entry into Internet classification.

There are many books banned in Australia (such as "E is for Ecstasy" or "Steal This Book") which are legal in most other English-speaking countries and the text of some is available on the Internet. To automatically classify contentious material of this sort as RC on the Internet would lead to absurd prosecutions. EFA submits that the decision in Michael Brown and Ors v. OFLC, to the extent that it may represent Australian law, is a matter for law reform by the Commonwealth and States. It could not be considered a reasonable position for the RC classification to extend to matters outside the Brandenburg v. Ohio definition:

> "Freedoms of speech and press do not permit a State to forbid advocacy of the use of force or of law violation except where such advocacy is directed to inciting or producing imminent lawless action and is likely to incite or produce such action."

As the decision presently stands, descriptions of Mahatma Gandhi's campaign of non-violent civil disobedience would be Refused Classification by the OFLC.

The potential for well-intentioned Australians, from teenagers to grandparents, to become unwitting victims of overzealous regulation is highly disturbing.

While it may be argued that Australians may have a reasonable understanding of what is permitted in publications and movies off-line from reading and viewing same, this is not actually a useful guide. For example, while the student editors of Rabelais were prosecuted for publishing material claimed to instruct in matters of crime, the August-September 1998 edition of Colors (the magazine of United Colors of Bennetton) included a six page article titled "Breaking and Entering".

This chapter contained interviews with "Technical Advisors", i.e. house breakers, and provided detailed instructions (including text and explanatory drawings) on how to break into houses. Attention was drawn to the article in the Sydney Morning Herald of 31 August 1998. Nevertheless that edition of Colors magazine was not banned, was not even classified and remained on sale, to both adults and children, in Australian newsagents.

On the global Internet, users may access a wide range of material which would be banned on Australian sites, yet Governments plan to expect them to know that they may be penalised under criminal law for publishing the same or similar information.

One wonders whether university students, for example, would realise that making available a thesis documenting in detail torture in prisons may be a criminal offence on grounds that it "instructs in matters of crime". In the event such content would not be refused classification, it is not likely to escape being rated "unsuitable for minors" requiring access to be subject to an approved restricted access system. In any case, what justification can reasonably be presented for punishing Australians who make available such material, while academics in other countries may make such material available to anyone on the Internet. While the OFLC is required to consider educational merit as well as protection of minors from material likely to harm or disturb them, it will be a matter of sheer guesswork for content providers as to which aspect would take precedence in the opinion of a majority of the members of the OFLC Classification Board.

Applying guidelines for movies to written text on the Internet has the distinct potential to result in absurd prosecutions for making available information in books and other publications that are not restricted off-line.

EFA calls on the NSW Parliament not to enter into Internet regulation intended to criminalise NSW people using classifications so inflexible and simplistic as those developed for movies and publications.

While claims may be made that offence provisions will only be used and/or prosecuted in the most exceptional cases of undoubted criminality, EFA submits that this is improperly relying on the discretion of police and prosecutors to apply a bad law.

In the case of the student editors of Rabelais, after some 4 years, and much public criticism of the decision to press charges, the Director of Public Prosecutions dropped the charges without explanation. It is preferable that bad laws enabling ludicrous prosecutions, and associated waste of taxpayers' funds, not be enacted in the first place.

Applicability issues

Drafting error enables prosecution of persons intended to be exempt

Clause 45B(2) makes the Bill apply to persons to whom it is not intended to apply because the phrasing of the exemption clause does not correspond exactly to the relevant offences under the Bill. The clause states:

"Nothing in this Part makes it an offence to supply objectionable matter or matter unsuitable for minors by means of an on-line service to any person, or class of persons, prescribed by the regulations."

The South Australian Select Committee recommended the above clause be amended and the SA Bill has been amended (but had not been passed by the SA House of Assembly as at January 2002). EFA recommends the same amendment be made to the NSW Bill.

Non-exclusive application of Part / potential unintended consequences

Prosecution of Librarians, Teachers, Internet Cafes

Clause 45B(3) appears intended to pr ovide protection from criminal proceedings to persons who may make material available in circumstances beyond their control. However, it is inadequate due to definitional problems and/or the effect of insertion of the clause into the existing Classification Act. The clause states:

45B (3) A person is not guilty of an offence under this Part by reason only of the person:

(a) owning, or having the control and management of the operation of, an on-line service, or

(b) facilitating access to or from an on-line service by means of transmission, down loading, intermediate storage, access software or similar capabilities.

While the above clause may provide adequate protection in relation to offences under Schedule 2 of the Bill, it appears unlikely to provide adequate protection to persons such as librarians, teachers, parents and managers of Internet cafes in relation to offences under the existing Act that may be committed as a result of facilitating access to or from an on-line service.

Schedule 2 defines proscribed matter as "Internet content consisting of...a film or computer game" that is or would be classified R, X or RC. The definition of a "film" in the existing Act states:

> "film includes...and any other form of recording from which a visual image, including a computer generated image, can be produced"

If this definition of "film" includes text and static images on Web pages, as appears intended by Schedule 2, then under the existing Act librarians and teachers (and others) who manage or supervise premises containing computers connected to the Internet can be prosecuted for screening films, that is, web pages.

In this regard the existing NSW Classification Act includes the following:

> 'exhibit a film (or an advertisement for a film) means project or screen the film or advertisement'

There is no doubt that a web page is "screened" on a computer monitor.

> 'public place means any place which the public is entitled to use or which is open to or used by the public, whether on payment of money or otherwise'

The definition of "public place" certainly covers libraries, some (perhaps all) schools and Internet cafes.

Under the existing Act, it is an offence to publicly exhibit (i.e. screen) an unclassified film (i.e. web page) or films (i.e. web pages) classified in a particular way:

'6. ...public exhibition of unclassified, RC or X films prohibited A person must not sell or publicly exhibit:

(a) a film classified RC or X, or

(b) an unclassified film.'

Hence, under the existing Act, it is illegal to screen any "film", i.e. web page, that is not classified. It is also illegal to screen some films that are classified. Therefore, a librarian, teacher or Internet cafe staff member who merely has superintendence or management of a public place where an unclassified web page (film) is screened (exhibited) is apparently in breach of the law. Since the vast majority of Internet content is not classified and is unlikely to ever be classified, merely providing a computer that screens any Web page appears to be a criminal offence. While the potential for such a prosecution may not immediately seem significant, it is a different matter when one considers that, for example, pornography may be inadvertently displayed on computer screen while a mother and child are accessing the Internet in a library. While this is beyond the control of the manager or supervisor of the library, and neither the BSA or proposed NSW legislation will make the slightest difference to the possibility, there is no apparent impediment to prosecution of persons who merely have superintendence or management of premises in which a film/web page is exhibited/screened by another person.

EFA submits that if it is contended that the above persons could not be prosecuted because a web page is not a film under the existing Act, then a web page is also not a film under Schedule 2 of the Bill as the definition of a film is the same in both instances. Therefore content providers/Internet users could not be prosecuted for making available a web page because it would not be "Internet content that consists of a film".

If Internet content such as a Web page is a film, then those providing access to the uncensorable Internet must be protected from prosecution for State and Federal offences under all Parts of the existing Act.

Prosecution of Parents and Guardians

Other sections of the existing Act present the potential for parents and guardians to face criminal proceedings for accidentally privately exhibiting Web pages/films in the presence of their children. For example, Clause 14 states:

> 14(1) A person must not privately exhibit in the presence of a minor a film classified RC or X or an unclassified film that would, if classified, be classified RC or X. Maximum penalty: 100 penalty units.

Since the legislation is claimed to be necessary on the ground that parents cannot control their own and/or their children's access to the Internet, it is unreasonable to enable their prosecution should material on the world wide Internet be inadvertently accessed and screened in their home.

Prosecution for Sale of Unclassified Material, e.g. newspaper articles, online

If a Web page containing text and static images is a "film" under the Act (as discussed above) then commercial content providers such as the Sydney Morning Herald are in breach of the existing NSW (and other State/Territory) Classification Act whether or not the web pages ("films") they make available are objectionable matter or matter unsuitable for minors.

Newspaper publishers presently sell electronic copies of newspaper articles online, via provision of a Web page/"film" containing the article, without having the article (Web page/ "film") classified prior to sale. It is an offence in NSW and all other States/Territories under existing Acts to sell an unclassified film.

Restricted Access Systems

Availability and Suitability of Systems

There is considerable misunderstanding concerning the defence of an approved restricted access system. As detailed in Section 6.9 above, it is apparent that some legislators have no understanding whatsoever regarding the nature of the Internet, as distinct from a cinema or licensed premises, and hence the privacy and security issues involved in requiring users to provide proof of age online, and furthermore have failed to grasp that the proposed legislation requires the use of "an approved", not "a", restricted access system.

The Bill refers to "approved restricted access system" which is defined as follows:

45D (3) In this section:

approved restricted access system means:

(a) a restricted access system within the meaning of the Broadcasting Services Act 1992 of the Commonwealth; or

(b) any other system of limiting access declared by the Minister, by order published in the Gazette, to be an approved restricted access system for the purposes of this definition.

While the NSW Bill gives the State Minister power to approve a restricted access system, the BSA does not recognise systems approved by a State Minister, only those approved by the ABA. Hence content on the Internet can be ordered taken down under the BSA even if access to it is subject to a system approved by the NSW Minister.

In the two years since the Commonwealth Parliament passed the BSA, only one "restricted access system" has been approved under that Act by the ABA.

The system is administratively onerous to the extent that few Australian content hosts would be prepared to incur the costs involved in setting up the relevant systems.

The system is extraordinarily privacy intrusive, requiring users to provide personal identifying information that goes far beyond proof of age, while not meeting the objective of protecting children more effectively than standard restricted access systems presently in use.

Identification details are easily forged, demonstrating conventional wisdom that effective age- authentication systems are almost impossible to implement on the Internet. The system is totally out of step with the essential character of the Internet as a public communication medium.

Information about other presently available "restricted access systems" (that have not been "approved") is provided below.

EFA submits that there is a fundamental misunderstanding among policy makers and legislators as to the type of restricted access systems presently available which claim to restrict access to particular content on the Internet to adults.

While these systems require Internet users to enter a PIN number or password (Adult Check type services), or a credit card number, in order to access material, they do not prevent children from accessing the material, however they do infringe adults' privacy.

Access by PIN Number/Password ("Adult Check" Type Services)

Many providers of sexually explicit material require users to pay a fee to a different service provider for a PIN number or password prior to being granted access to material on their site. The providers of these PIN numbers/passwords pay web site operators a percentage of the fee paid by the user. Web site operators place an advertisement for the PIN number/password service on their own site. When users click on this advert to go the other site, the PIN number provider receives notification of the site the user was visiting and thus knows which web site operator to pay for the business/referral. Use of such systems by web site providers is as likely to be a money making exercise as a claimed means of keeping children away from their content.

Providers of PIN numbers/passwords advertise that these are instantly available on filling in a web form and providing a credit card number for payment. It is thus highly unlikely that the providers verify that the user of the credit card is an adult at any time, let alone before they are provided with a PIN number/password and thereby granted access to material, nor is it apparent how they could verify the user's age. Most, probably all, providers of PIN numbers/passwords are located outside Australia, although they do provide PIN numbers/passwords to Australians.

It is clearly impossible for any PIN number/password provider, ISP or content provider to know who is actually at the other end of an Internet carriage service line applying for a PIN/number password or accessing a web site using same.

Some banks provide credit cards to minors and minors may "borrow" a credit card number from their parents unbeknown to them. While parents may notice an authorised charge of some $20 on their credit card bill, this may not occur until some two months after the PIN number/password was provided. During that time harm, if any, that may be suffered by minors in accessing R-rated content will likely have occurred.

Moreover, without unauthorised use of a credit card, minors may be told of a PIN number/password by friends, or may obtain a PIN number/password from lists available on web sites.

Access by Credit Card Number

Another form of "restricted access system" is to require users to provide a credit card number prior to accessing content. This is presently used only by commercial sites who require payment for products or services. While the marketing model works for popular adult sexually explicit sites, it is well known that Internet users will rarely pay (regardless of their financial circumstances) to access other information.

The proposition that non-commercial Australian sites commence requiring credit card numbers presents a number of problems.

Extra features such as scripting and server configuration are required to implement systems restricting access to persons providing credit card numbers. Most content providers do not have the technical knowledge or funding to set up such systems themselves.

Furthermore, the technology necessary to implement such systems is often unavailable to small content providers whose content is hosted by ISP/ICHs who do not offer them the technical means to restrict access due to technical and security issues, costs, etc.

In cases where either the content provider or their ISP/ICH is technically and financially able to restrict access by requiring credit card numbers other problems arise.

Legislation provides for the declaration of "approved restricted access systems" and requires providers of R-rated content to use such systems. If, for example, a system requiring users to enter a credit card number was approved, there is no requirement for the content provider to check the validity of the credit card number or the age of the user of the credit card. In such a circumstance, an Internet user may enter any group of 16 digits.

If the approved system includes a requirement that the content provider check that the credit card number complies with the check algorithm, an Internet user may simply download one of the credit card number generator algorithms freely available on the Internet and create a number.

If the approved system includes a requirement that the content provider or ISP/ICH check that the credit card number belongs to a bona fide account, then government will need to legislate that banks and other credit card providers must provide free-of-charge services to verify validity of credit card numbers in cases where no sale is to take place. It is highly questionable whether banks and other credit card providers will greet such a government requirement with enthusiasm, however absent their co-operation there is no means by which persons providing content free-of-charge are able to verify the bona-fides of a credit card number.

In circumstances when the bona-fides of a credit card number can be verified, Internet users, both adults and minors, may use credit card numbers belonging to their parents, relatives, friends, enemies, employers or indeed politicians should they happen to have that information. Since no sale is taking place, the misuse of credit card numbers is unlikely to be identified by the owner of the credit card. Meanwhile a trail suggesting they have accessed numerous sites of varying content will be left around the Web.

Privacy

Australians have long evidenced serious concerns about their privacy. Almost all web traffic consists of private communications - personal access to information. Users expect privacy for this in the same way that they expect their library borrowing records to be private or their magazine purchases to be largely anonymous.

Requiring users to obtain and use PIN numbers/ passwords, or provide credit card numbers, enhances the ability of ISPs, web site operators, etc., to monitor and track Internet users' activities and interests. It may therefore result in such information, as well as their personal information provided to obtain a PIN number/password, being used for marketing and other purposes without their knowledge or permission.

Furthermore, the Bill provides no privacy protection for personal information provided by Internet users to web sites and the Commonwealth Privacy Act excludes content hosts and content providers whose turnover is under $3 million per year.

Ease of Finding Australian Content

Search engines do not index material protected by access controls. Small sites that cannot afford advertising depend on search engines to draw visitors. Many sites contain content that would be rated in different categories. Without the resources to classify their content, content providers will be forced to take the safe option and "protect" the entire site, thus restricting access to material which is not even R-rated. This will result in it being difficult for adults to find information they seek. Information on non-Australian sites will be easier to find than Australian content.

Effectiveness in Protecting Minors

EFA submits that the proposed mandatory use of "restricted access systems" (approved or otherwise) in relation to material that is or would be classified R presents more problems than it solves. In fact, it does not solve any problem.

Commonwealth and proposed NSW legislation does not provide any control whatsoever on overseas sites providing material that is or would be classified R. The imposition of access control systems on Australian sites will therefore have no effect on the unrestricted availability of R-rated material to minors, since it only affects the 1 or 2% of content hosted in Australia. In order to protect children from material that would be classified R, there will be an ongoing need for parents and educators to supervise the access of those in their care.

Regulation of R-rated content will cripple the Australian content-hosting industry and adversely affect Australian content providers. It will disproportionately hurt smaller, and particularly non-commercial, content providers.

Many, if not most, Internet users will not bother going through a verification procedure. On the Web, attention spans are short and barriers to access are low. Even a minor extra barrier will deter people. A simple registration requirement has this effect and a requirement to obtain and use an adult ID, with all the privacy concerns that raises, will deter almost all visitors who will instead access overseas sites.

Content providers will opt to host their content overseas, where they simply do not have to worry about attempting to restrict access. They will either use one of the many overseas services that host content free of charge, or pay overseas services to host their content. In cases where the content is not illegal under the laws of the country where the content is hosted (e.g. R, X and some RC material is not illegal in the USA), it is questionable whether content hosts would disclose identifying information about their customers' to Australian law enforcement authorities.

Enforcing the use of "restricted access systems" will be the death knell for Australian content (in Australia) which requires an "adult perspective" but does not contain pornography or violence. Meanwhile minors will continue to have unrestricted access to material provided by non-Australian content providers that would be classified R.

The BSA enables the taking down of R-classified material by ICH/ISPs. There is no benefit in criminalising Australian content providers, or attempting to restrict content and conversation on the Australian Internet to that fit for a kindergarten, when similar material will be readily available to children on overseas sites.

Australia's International Obligations

There is a disturbing trend towards an increasingly repressive censorship regime in all media in Australia. While such measures invariably claim "protecting the children" as an objective, they deny the rights of adult Australians to read, see and hear what they want and they deny parents' responsibility for safeguarding their children.

The Internet censorship legislation is a primary example. It will not achieve the claimed aim of protecting children, but it will infringe adults' rights to freedom of speech and the legislated principle in Australian law that adults should be free to read, see and hear what they want.

The legislation contravenes Australia's international obligations as a signatory to the Universal Declaration of Human Rights and the International Covenant on Civil and Political Rights (ICCPR). The ICCPR forms Schedule 2 of the Human Rights and Equal Opportunity Commission Act 1986. Article 19 of the ICCPR states:

1. Everyone shall have the right to hold opinions without interference.
2. Everyone shall have the right to freedom of expression; this right shall include freedom to seek, receive and impart information and ideas of all kinds, regardless of frontiers, either orally, in writing or in print, in the form of art, or through any other media of his choice.
3. The exercise of the rights provided for in paragraph 2 of this article carries with it special duties and responsibilities. It may therefore be subject to certain restrictions, but these shall only be such as are provided by law and are necessary:

(a) For respect of the rights or reputations of others;

(b) For the protection of national security or of public order, or of public health or morals.

EFA draws to attention that the legislation will infringe the rights of Australian citizens under clause 19(2) and is not "necessary" as set out in clause 19(3).

While Commonwealth and proposed NSW legislation will restrict Australian's freedom of speech and may inconvenience them in accessing content on the Internet, they will be wholly unsuccessful in terms of protection of "national security or of public order, or of public health or morals" since they have no effect on material available to Australians on off-shore web sites.

The Internet is a world-wide communication system which all Australian Governments must accept they cannot control, just as other Western democracies have. The restrictions on freedom to seek, receive and impart information and ideas of all kinds will not be mitigated by the tiny quantity of information on a global network that Australian Governments' censorship regime might successfully ban.

The Bill is clearly premature in its attempt to impose a classification regime on the Internet when there are no adequate procedures in place to classify such content (nor at a cost affordable to many ordinary Australians) and there are strong doubts that the use of film guidelines are appropriate to this medium.

Numerous difficulties are likely to arise in attempting to enforce the proposed law, including the matter of constitutional validity.

Moreover, the Bill is out of step with world opinion on Internet content regulation.

The physical location of Internet content is a matter of little relevance. A content provider in any Australian State or Territory can have content hosted elsewhere in Australia or any other country. Realistically, to deny Australian content hosts the right to host content legal and protected elsewhere is to make Australian sites uniquely disadvantaged in a global market.

EFA strongly supports the principle that content creators rather than carriage service providers should be responsible for online content, and that criminal culpability for such content should apply only to material that is globally and unequivocally recognised as illegal.

All commentators accept that there is some Internet content that is universally condemned, and some consider international efforts to eradicate it are capable of success. EFA submits that seeking to achieve global agreement on the definition would be an appropriate response by all Australian Governments intent on making an effective contribution to dealing with criminal content. Obviously, the narrowest definitions of illegal content are most likely to be successfully prohibited - a wide definition that includes material routinely available in other countries and protected as free speech in the United States (such as material classified R and X and much of material Refused Classification in Australia) would be pointless and unenforceable. International agencies such as Interpol have no interest in investigating erotica, nor the wide range of material classified "R"/"unsuitable for minors" under Australian censorship laws.

The oft-quoted issue of "protection of minors from exposure to material that may be harmful to them" invites debate over the means to that end. In the event that parents consider that filtering Internet content is a desirable alternative to adequately teaching minors to deal with all types of Internet content, this is best achieved with personally chosen software programs and services and proper supervision appropriate to age and maturity. The provisions of the Commonwealth BSA already require Internet Service Providers to provide their customers with an Approved Filter, that is, approved under the ISP Code of Practice registered by the Australian Broadcasting Authority.

The increasing emergence of specialist content providers for children will reduce the need for supervision in some cases. Minors are not all impressionable victims nor hardened hackers, and parents are better placed than Governments to determine whether a problem exists with their child's use of the Internet. The development of a range of online services and market forces are a better means of giving parents control over their children's activities.

As President Clinton resolved, following the defeat of the Communications Decency Act, it is the role of the police to track down paedophiles and terrorists - and it is up to parents to supervise their child's use of the Internet.

Existing classification legislation and laws of general application enable State and Territory police to prosecute persons engaged in child abuse and terrorism who may use the Internet just as they use the telephone, mail and roads. If there is a problem in enforcing existing laws, EFA contends that this is most likely to be associated with insufficient liaison between Commonwealth and State and Territory police forces and insufficient funding of police for training purposes and resources necessary to track down criminals who use the Internet. EFA recommends that funds proposed to be used in enacting and enforcing the proposed legislation to criminalise merely controversial speech instead be directed to increased funding of police forces.

Publication of globally agreed illegal material can already be prosecuted under existing NSW law (such as the Crimes Act Sec 578C - "Publishing child pornography and indecent articles"), and regulations concerning contentious material are inappropriate in a world where cultural differences cannot be easily reconciled.

Index